Criminal Justice

Recent Scholarship

Edited by
Marilyn McShane and Frank P. Williams III

A Series from LFB Scholarly

The Use of Force by Detention Officers

Marie L. Griffin

LFB Scholarly Publishing LLC
New York 2001

Library of Congress Cataloging-in-Publication Data

Griffin, Marie L.
 The use of force by detention officers / Marie L. Griffin.
  p. cm. -- (Criminal justice recent scholarship)
 Includes bibliographical references and index.
  ISBN 1-931202-01-X (alk. paper)
  1. Inmate guards--Arizona--Maricopa County--Case studies. 2.
 Prison violence--Arizona--Maricopa County--Case studies. I.
 Title. II. Series.
  HV9481.M36 G75 2001
  365'.64--dc21

2001003992

ISBN 1-931202-01-X

Printed on acid-free 250-year-life paper.

Manufactured in the United States of America.

Table of Contents

v

Tables

Figures

CHAPTER 1
Introduction

Described alternatively as "conflict ridden social worlds" (Jacobs, 1983), "the sewers of the justice system" (Houston, Gibbons & Jones, 1988), "dirty little worlds" (Stohr, Lovrich, Menke & Zupan, 1994) and institutions where "idleness, overcrowding, deteriorating physical facilities, and inadequate medical and psychiatric treatment ... contribute to the instability and negative social climate" (Bowker, 1982, p. 319), jails generally are relegated to the lowest level of status among social institutions, receiving only limited attention from social science research. Additionally, it has been noted that "the largest gap in the literature on jails is the lack of study of their day-to-day operations" (Senese & Kalinich, 1993, p. 132).

Jails are coercive organizations, and even routine interactions between officers and inmates take place within an environment of structured conflict. Given the officer's need to maintain control over inmates, the use or threatened use of force by detention officers against inmates is a routine part of daily operations. While force is more effective for social control if constantly available but seldom used (Hepburn, 1985), officers must be ready to use force to gain compliance.

The extent to which the use or threatened use of force is essential to the functioning of correctional institutions may be debated, however the basic coercive nature of the institution cannot be ignored. As Etzioni (1977) argues,

> Force is the major means of control applied in these organizations to assure fulfillment of the major organizational task: keeping inmates in. Obviously, should the restraints on movement be lifted, hardly any inmate would stay inside. The accomplishment of all other tasks depends on the effective performance of this custodial task...even when control relies directly on other means, indirectly it is based on force. (p. 9)

Broader issues regarding the basic principles of modern punishment and fundamental questions regarding the right to punish are relevant to any discussion of punishment, imprisonment and control, but the appropriate use of state sanctioned force is not the focus of this study. Instead, this research examines the nature of the jail organization, and the resulting attitudes of detention officers regarding use of force.

While the study of the use of force within the criminal justice system as a whole has grown considerably over the past 30 years, the main body of research regarding use of force is found in policing, primarily focusing on police officers' use of deadly force (Riksheim & Chermak, 1993). With very few exceptions (Marquart, 1986), little attention has been paid to detention officers and their use of force against inmates. This is a glaring oversight given that prisons and jails are coercive organizations in which the use of force, or the threatened use of force, in the control of inmates is a regular occurrence. As the literature on police use of force provides only limited insight into the use of force by detention officers, the need for research regarding use of force in the correctional setting grows ever more important.

This dearth of research on use of force by detention officers requires an examination of predictors of other types of officer behavior and attitudes within the correctional setting. A great deal of research does focus on the attitudes and behaviors of the detention officer and his or her role within the correctional organization. Organizational climate research has occupied a popular position in industrial and organizational psychology for a number of years, and is currently a growing interest to researchers examining the relationship between correctional environment and behavioral outcomes and attitudes. Specifically, the work environment, comprised of numerous climates within which an individual functions, has been identified as a significant predictor of a variety of behaviors and attitudes (e.g., job satisfaction, professional orientation, role stress) (Chase, 1973; Litwin & Stringer, 1968; Moos, 1975; Porter, Lawler & Hackman, 1975; Pritchard & Karasick, 1973; Robinson et al., 1997; Schneider, 1975; Smith & Ivester, 1987). It is generally accepted that an organizational environment possesses many climates "representing prevailing conditions of the organizational environment as related to characteristics of the job, the leadership, the workgroup and the various subsystems as well as the total organization" (James and Jones, 1976, p. 100). These specific climates within an institution, as perceived by the individual, "emerge from a person's daily activities, interactions and experiences within the organization" (Sneider & Hall, 1972, p. 448), influencing and directing the attitudes and behavior of the individuals. Climate acts as a critical link between the individual and the organization.

Generally, research regarding detention officers' attitudes and behaviors takes into consideration individual-level and work environment factors, suggesting that individuals, their work environment and the interaction between the two contribute significantly to the variance in behaviors (Barker, 1963; Engel and Moos, 1967; Gump et al., 1957; Moos, 1968; Moos and Daniel, 1967). More recent research indicates that the institutional climate in which officers operate is a much better predictor of officers' attitudes and behaviors than individual-level factors (Whitehead & Lindquist, 1989). However, research on the climate of correctional facilities often appears unclear and the findings ambiguous. Researchers often fail to frame their study within the broader context of organizational climate, neglecting the literature and findings from industrial and organizational psychology. This proves to be a serious shortcoming in correctional climate research, as such research fails to contribute to a more comprehensive understanding of the complicated relationship between the detention officer and the work environment.

While attention toward detention officers' attitudes and behavior in the context of climate continues to grow, use of force by officers as well as officer attitudes toward use of force are critical areas remaining relatively unexplored. With this in mind, the need to examine the routine exercise of force by correctional officers and its relation to a variety of climates within the correctional institution becomes apparent. This study proposes that correctional officers perceive conditions of the work environment, and that these perceptions, representing various climates within the institution, influence the attitudes and nature of the officers' interaction with or treatment of inmates, specifically an officer's readiness to use force against inmates.

CHAPTER 2
Use of Force and Organizational Climate

As noted previously, little research exists regarding use of force in corrections. Most use of force research is found in the policing literature, focusing on police officers' use of deadly force. Variables associated with police use of force generally are classified within three levels of analysis: individual variables (e.g., age, race, gender, tenure); situation variables (e.g., number of police present, suspect behavior, seriousness of offense) and organizational variables (e.g., style of policing, type of department) (Friedrich, 1980;Kavanagh, 1994; Riksheim & Chermak, 1993; Worden, 1996). Studies indicate that individual characteristics are less of a predictor of police use of force than are such situational factors as offender behavior or the presence or absence of citizens or other officers (Bayley & Garofalo, 1989; Friedrich, 1980; Hayden, 1981; Riksheim & Chermak, 1993; Sherman, 1980; Smith, 1986). In fact, when situational factors are controlled, individual level variables such as race, age, education and length of service have not been shown to significantly influence the use of force among police officers (Alpert, 1989; Friedrich, 1980; Hayden, 1981).

While significant in the analysis of police officer use of force, there is difficulty in directly transferring situational and organizational variables from a policing to a correctional setting. Few variables characterizing the nature of a policing situation (e.g., visibility, legal issues, seriousness) or a police organization (e.g., patrol strategy, department type: traditional, legalistic and progressive) are analogous to those situational and organizational variables characterizing a correctional setting[1.] For this reason, I do not address situational and organizational variables associated with police use of force, and instead discuss the relationship between individual level variables and police use of force, included in this analysis primarily to control for their effects.

Individual Variables

While exerting no direct influence, individual level variables such as race, gender, and tenure are found to be associated with police use of force.

Race

While most research indicates no significant direct relationship between race and an officer's use of force, findings vary. While race of an officer alone is found to have little effect on police use of force (Croft, 1985; Friedrich, 1980; Kavanagh, 1994), the use of racially mixed police teams appears "to exert a restraining effect," with force being used infrequently by such teams (Friedrich, 1980, p. 90). In other studies, a race effect is present, with minority officers less likely to use force than white officers

---

[1] Once exception is Marquart's (1986) study, which suggests that organizational structure, or the extent to which an organization is centralized or decentralized, influences guard aggression.

(Croft & Austin, 1987; Friedrich, 1980; Geller, 1980). Still other studies find black officers more likely to use force (Croft & Austin, 1987; Worden, 1992).

Gender

Most research regarding gender and an officer's use of force reports no significant relationship (Croft, 1985; Friedrich, 19980; Riksheim & Chermak, 1993). However, analyses of officer gender and use of deadly force reveal that females are less often involved in deadly force incidents (Horvath, 1987) and female officers working in male/female police teams are less likely to use deadly force than their male partners (Grennan, 1987).

Length of Service

While higher levels of experience have been hypothesized to lead to greater authoritarianism, and thus to more aggressive behavior (Niederhoffer, 1967), such a hypothesis finds little support in Friedrich's (1980) study of police use of force. On the contrary, "there is the slightest indication that more experienced officers use force more reasonably and less excessively than less experienced officers" (Friedrich, 1980, p. 89). Other research supports this position, finding that officers with more seniority were less likely to use force when attempting to control a suspect (Croft, 1985; Bayley & Garofalo, 1989).

Education

Although most studies have found little or no relationship between the level of education and a police officer's use of force (Croft, 1985; Friedrich, 1980;

Kavanagh, 1994), findings vary. Some studies indicate a negative relationship between education and use of force, with those officers with higher levels of education less likely to use force (Cascio, 1977; Cohen & Chaiken, 1972). However, Croft and Austin (1987) found officers with a four-year university degree more likely to use force.

Attitudinal Variables

In a review of police use of force research, Worden (1996) suggests that research in the area of attitudes and personality traits has been less rigorous and more limited than research addressing situational factors. In part, this may result from the findings of several social psychological studies which suggest that "attitudes and behaviors are related to an extent that ranges from small to moderate in degree" (Schuman & Johnson, 1976, p. 168). Worden (1987), for example, finds that the attitudes of police officers account for very little of the variation in their behavior as they performed basic law enforcement duties. More specifically, research attempting to link attitudes toward use of force and use of force behavior have found only a weak association. Attitudes toward use of force do not appear to be consistently related to actual use of force behavior (Ostrem et al., 1978).

Other researchers note the importance of attitudinal research and the need to further explore attitudes toward use of force and their correlates. Lester (1996) argues that "research does indicate that police officers have a great deal of variation in their attitudes (and their behavior), and this variation allows attitudinal theories to propose causal elements in police behavior" (p. 180). Some studies have explored the relationship between officer attitudes (other than toward use of force) and use of force behavior. A review of four studies incorporating the use of typologies of police officers finds that different types of officers appear to differ in their likelihood of using force (Worden, 1996). These typologies are based on attitudinal dimensions, including officers' "outlooks on human nature and their moral attitudes toward coercive authority" (Worden, 1996, p.26). However, these studies provide only weak support for the hypothesis that officer attitudes toward such issues as authority, officer roles and citizens are consistently related to use of force behaviors (Brown, 1981; Snipes & Mastrofski, 1990; Worden, 1989). In general, such research provides little support for the notion that behavior is consistently related to attitudes. Yet, it is important to note that such research does not completely discount attitudinal factors, instead suggesting that the relationship between behavior and attitudes is highly complex, arguably in need of further analysis (Worden, 1996).

Lester (1996) suggests the need to examine attitudes toward use of force, asking the question, "What other attitudes are associated with officers' attitudes toward the use of force, which personality traits, and which antecedent experiences (which might suggest hypotheses for the factors affecting the development of the attitudes)" (p. 188). Such a question redirects the focus of most use of force research, suggesting the need to deemphasize the relationship between attitudes and behavior and instead explore the way in which attitudes toward use of force are correlated with other job-related attitudes. A few studies have examined such correlates. Lester and Brink (1985) found that officers who were likely to report fellow officers for misuse of force also were likely to report fellow officers for a number of other behaviors, including drinking on duty, accepting free cups of coffee and accepting bribes. Other researchers have noted a negative correlation between job satisfaction and tolerance of physical and verbal abuse (Carter, 1976), as well as a positive relationship between fear of injury while on the job and a willingness to use authority to gain control of citizens (Corrigan et al., 1980). In addition, Lester et al. (1980) note that state police recruits who admit to greater expectations of danger on the job are less likely to view their job as one of helping citizens.

Organizational Climate Literature

Perhaps as a result of differing disciplines and approaches among researchers, a common or standard conception of 'climate' has yet to be achieved. Organizational climate has been called a "fuzzy concept" (Guion, 1973), one that "appears to be analogous with the organizational situation and, as such, is a 'catch-all' term" (James & Jones, 1974, p. 1099). Initial confusion stems from the haphazard labeling of the organizational situation (structures, policies, procedures and practices) which comprises the work environment and is perceived by those individuals functioning within the organization. Climate literature is littered with such terms as "social climate" (Houston et al., 1988; Wright, 1980; Wright & Boudouris, 1982), "work environment" (Camp, 1994), "environmental factors" (Wenk & Moos, 1972), "organizational culture" (Schein, 1990), "employee perceptions" (Furnham & Gunter, 1994), "psychological climate" (James, 1982; James & Jones, 1976), "organizational climate" (Bedeian, Armenakis & Curran, 1981; Guzley, 1992; Hershberger,

Lichtenstein & Knox, 1994; Payne, 1990), "perceived work environment" (James & Jones, 1980) and "context" (Blau, Light & Chamlin, 1986). Such terms generally, but not necessarily, refer to similar conceptions of the work environment. Too often, studies fail to specify a theoretical model, neglecting issues of measurement and causality. Yet, all is not chaos. As Tagiuri (1968) notes:

> It is clear that the term [climate] is used in widely disparate contexts. Yet each time it refers to some feature or characteristic of the environment that has consequences for the behavior of an individual or group, and to which the person is somehow sensitive. (p. 18)

Generally Agreed Upon Climate Issues

This issue of inconsistent labeling merely touches the surface of a much larger debate concerning what climate actually represents and, in turn, how to best measure the concept of climate. In an attempt to address such confusing conceptual issues, it is necessary to examine various theoretical conceptions of climate outlined primarily in industrial and organizational psychology literature and the way in which it has come to be employed in current correctional research.

A Definition of Climate

While several issues are key in the debate over the conceptualization of climate, complicating the development and operationalization of a systematic framework within which to study organizational behavior, a consensus on a general definition has evolved over time. Early researchers described climate in terms of the 'personality' or 'character' of the organizational environment (Moos, 1975; Selsnick, 1957). More specifically, a climate is said to be defined by a set of characteristics which "(a) distinguishes the organization from other organizations, (b) are relatively enduring over time, and (c) influence the behavior of people in the organization" (Forehand & Gilmer, 1964, p. 362). Added to this is the general belief that climates are perceived by individuals and are psychological in nature (James, Hater, Gent & Bruni, 1978; Jones & James, 1979; Joyce & Slocum, 1979; Schneider, 1975; Schneider & Rentsch, 1988; Weick, 1979). Schneider (1975) provides a definition of climate, emphasizing the largely psychological nature of climate:

> Climate perceptions are psychologically meaningful... descriptions that people can agree characterize a system's practices and procedures. By its practices and procedures a system may create many climates. People perceive climates because the...perceptions function as frames of reference for the attainment of some congruity between behavior and the system's practices and procedures. However, if the climate is one which rewards and supports the display of individual differences, people in the same system will not behave similarly. (p. 475)

A final component of a definition of climate addresses the influence of individual perceptions of the work environment. Most climate theorists agree that perceptions significantly influence organizational outcomes and behavior such as productivity, performance, satisfaction and personal growth. After an extensive review of the climate literature, Pritchard and Karasick (1973) offer the following definition of climate, incorporating all generally agreed upon assumptions of climate research. According to Pritchard and Karasick (1973), climate is:

...a relatively enduring quality of an organization's internal environments distinguishing it from other organizations; (a)which results from the behavior and policies of members of the organization, especially management; (b) which is perceived by members of the organization; (c) which serves as a basis for interpreting the situation; and (d) acts as a source of pressure for directing activity. (p. 127)

Beyond this fundamental description, the further clarification of the concept of climate becomes less and less consistent. Numerous yet often conflicting elaborations are suggested, though rarely placed within a broader theoretical framework. As a result, the concept of 'climate' expands in an incoherent manner, often leaving the complexity of questions regarding operationalization, measurement and analysis unanswered. Indik (1968) addresses this point, noting that:

Without an acceptable basic rationale for an underlying systematic taxonomic framework, knowledge in the area of organizational behavior will continue to proliferate in a fragmentary and unorganized manner. It will continue to seem too massive in its amount, contradictory in substance, simple-minded, fragmentary, and ungeneralizable. (p. 4)

Organizational Climate Research and the Climates Within

Schneider (1975) attempts to clarify a basic issue of terminology by drawing a distinction between 'organizational climate' and 'climates'. Schneider suggests that the term 'organizational climate' should be used in reference to a general area of research. The term 'climate' should be used to refer to one of any number of climates which exists within an organization, with each climate possessing its own particular set of dimensions. That is, the concept of climate is multidimensional, in that as many types of climates exist in an organization as are there are areas of interest. For example, Schneider, Parkington & Buxton (1980) studied the 'service climate' of banks, Coleman (1961) researched the climate of 'academic achievement' in high schools, Stohr et al. (1994) studied the climate associated with the 'Employee Investment Model' of jail management, Zohar (1980) evaluated the 'safety' climate of industrial organizations, Moos (1975) looked at the three climates of 'relationships', 'personal development and growth' and 'system maintenance and system change' within psychiatric treatment programs.

James and Jones (1976) also attempt to clarify the concept of climate, noting the existence of two different types of climates -- the organizational climate and the psychological climate. James and Jones (1976) suggest an expanded model of organizational functioning, with a conceptual distinction being made between organizational climate (prevailing conditions of the organizational environment), psychological climate (perceptions of prevailing conditions of the organizational environment), and organizationally related attitudes (affective responses to climate, such as job satisfaction). The nature of the relationship among these components is further defined, wherein organizationally related attitudes are described as being relatively "susceptible to change as a function of the experiences in the organization, and...they provide an operationalization of the intervening psychological process..." (James & Jones, 1976, p. 100). This framework serves as an important, yet preliminary, step in the development of a comprehensive framework within which to study climate. However, James and Jones (1976) use of the term 'organizational climate' conflicts with that of Schneider (1975), providing another example of the lack of standardization in terminology, a problem characteristic of climate literature.

Levels of Analysis

A final feature of climate on which there exists some consensus is the different levels at which to discuss climate. Analysis of climate is generally considered to take place at the psychological or individual level, the group or subsystem level, the organizational or structural level and the socio-cultural or external level (Indik, 1968; James & Jones, 1974; Joyce & Slocum, 1982; Rentsch, 1990; Saylor, 1992).

Unresolved Climate Issues

While a consensus on a general definition of climate exists and issues of terminology are somewhat easily addressed, the complexity of dealing with several levels of analysis introduces a certain amount of confusion. A number of issues relating to the representation of climate, its operationalization and analysis continue to muddy climate literature.

Organizational Attributes Of Climate

The focus now turns from a general definition of climate to those attributes that represent climate and those variables which measure climate. One issue central to the development of a comprehensive theoretical framework centers on what climate actually represents. Is climate an attribute of the organization or the individual? Debate continues as to whether climate is a property of the organization, the result of the individuals comprising the organization, or the "joint property of both the organization and the individual" (Ashforth, 1985, p. 838). At issue is whether climate represents objective (physical or structural) characteristics of the organization or the subjective (perceptual) response to the organization, or an integration of both of these measures.

Climate often is measured through responses to survey questions which are then "interpreted as measuring the extent to which the individual interprets the organizational environment as possessing a particular quality" (Rentsch, 1990, p. 669). The concern, therefore, lies in the fact that most measures of climate are based on subjective perceptions of the individual and not an objective description of the work environment. However, many climate theorists have come to agree that the unique character of an organization or group is the result of the total and direct daily interactions between the individual and the organization, and as such there exists a need to develop integrated models for organizational research which "encompass both individual and situation characteristics as antecedent causes of individual behavior and attitudes in organizational settings" (James & Jones, 1976, p. 76). Yet, some climate theorists continue to view climate solely as the property of the organization (Forehand & Gilmer, 1964; Payne & Pugh, 1976; Wright & Boudouris, 1982).

Perception Vs. Structure: The Subjective/Objective Dichotomy

Recent studies (Saylor, 1984; Saylor, 1992; Saylor & Gilman, 1992) continue to focus on the subjective/objective dichotomy of the climate debate, unnecessarily shifting the emphasis of climate research to this distinction. Such a dichotomy does more to circumvent the complexity of the relationships among the several levels of analysis than to add clarity. For example, Saylor (1984) offers this dichotomy as framework for measuring organizational climates:

> the "subjective" (also referred to as "psychological" or "process") approach in which responses are collected from individual members of organizations and then aggregated to yield measures of organizations as a whole, and the "objective" (also referred to as "organizational or "structural") approach wherein organizational level information is gleaned from organizational records. (p. 1)

Perhaps Saylor (1984) utilizes this dichotomy to further distinguish the nature of aggregated data. However, many climate theorists have addressed this issue of aggregation and would argue there exists little need to introduce the subjective/objective distinction as a foundation for an analytical framework (Indik, 1968; James, 1982).

Suggested Theoretical Frameworks for Climate Analysis

Arguing that the subjective/objective dichotomy is merely an additional layer of terminology which oversimplifies complex issues of analysis, James (1982) contends that what is of importance is not "whether perception is involved in the measurement process (if humans are involved in the measurement, then perceptions is necessarily involved), rather the question should be about the nature of the variable measured" (p. 220). James (1982) maintains that "the unit(s) on which a theory is based (i.e. units of theory) should dictate the units selected for observation" (p. 220). If one is interested in structural characteristics of an organization, such as the number of hierarchical levels, the ratio of inmates to officers or the security level, then obviously the unit of analysis should be the organization. However, if one is interested in how organizational characteristics, policies or procedures influence an individual's behavior or attitude, then the unit of analysis is the individual.

Where Saylor's (1984) subjective/objective approach falters is with his labeling of aggregated individual level perceptions. With his approach, Saylor (1984) describes "collective perceptions" as one example of "objective institutional level measures" (p. 2). Keeping in mind that these collective perceptions are based on individual perceptions, which represent subjective characterizations of a particular facet of the work environment, confusion arises as to whether a 'collective perception' is truly an objective or subjective measure. Saylor does not address this issue. However, some climate theorists take issue with the use of aggregated data to represent climate at the organizational level (Hershberger et al., 1994; James, 1982; Rentsch, 1990; Selo, 1976; Wright & Boudouris, 1982). This focus on objective versus subjective approach unnecessarily introduces yet another layer of climate language and serves to bypass the critical and often complex relationship among the various levels of measurement.

Indik (1968) also emphasizes the need to focus on level of measurement and not perception versus structure, suggesting that a logical theoretical framework begin with the four levels of analysis (individual, group, organization and socio-cultural environment) within which variables are subcategorized and then distinguishing between those variables that are structural in nature and those that are dynamic. What Saylor (1984) might define as subjective or objective variables are integrated appropriately at each level of Indik's (1968) classification system. With such a scheme, Indik (1968) hopes that perhaps there can be a "reduction in the amount of semantic confusion engendered by calling the same variable by different names and by using the same names for different variables" (p. 26). Although James (1982), Saylor (1984) and Indik (1968) suggest differing classification systems, each represents an effort to integrate both individual level and organizational level variables into a broader framework within which to study climate. The effort to develop an integrated framework introduces a certain amount of complexity, however it is a critical step toward understanding the influence of both macro and micro organizational characteristics on organizational behavior and attitudes.

An Issue of Aggregation

While the issue of aggregation has been touched upon briefly in the discussion of different levels of analysis, a more thorough treatment of the subject is warranted. The debate over the validity of aggregate data is difficult to separate from earlier discussions regarding the appropriate level of analysis for climate research. The objective/subjective dichotomy, concern over what climate actually represents and the issue of aggregate data is interrelated. As noted previously, climate is generally characterized as a mediating or intervening variable which describes the conditions within an organization, as perceived by the individual, and which in turn influences individual attitudes and behavior. Researchers address the issue of perceptual and structural variables at the individual level, the group level, the organizational level and the socio-cultural level. However, a critical question dealing with measurement remains unresolved. Is it possible to move from one level of analysis to the next, wherein data from one level are used to characterize attributes of another? More specifically, to what extent do aggregated perceptions of individuals constitute a valid measure of the organization? The use of aggregated perceptual scores, in addition to situational factors (size, security level or number of hierarchical levels) is a potentially powerful tool to explain organizational behavior and attitudes. However, debate continues at to the validity of such scores.

It is argued that if aggregated responses of individuals do in fact represent or characterize some attribute of the entire organization, then it must be assumed that individuals interpret the organization in a similar manner (Rentsch, 1990). However, many climate researchers are uncomfortable with the notion of a global or shared perception, arguing different people perceive situations differently (Payne, 1990; Wright & Boudouris, 1982). This is the point upon which the debate over the use of aggregated data turns. As James and Jones (1974) note,

> It is somewhat confusing if one wishes to employ organizational climate as an organizational attribute or main effect, since the use of perceptual measurement introduces variance which is a function of the differences between individuals and is not necessarily descriptive of organizations or structures. Therefore accuracy and/or consensus of perceptions must be verified if accumulated perceptual organizational climate measures are used to describe organizational attributes. (p. 1103)

Other researchers acknowledge the critical need for verification of consensus among individual perceptions and suggest that aggregate scores meet certain criteria to avoid aggregation bias (James, 1982; Jones & James, 1979; Roberts, Hulin & Rousseau, 1978).[2] When one attempts to translate directly the characteristics or properties from one level of analysis to another, there is the potential for aggregation bias. Aggregation bias exists when "estimates of agreement based on group mean scores [are] incorrectly interpreted as applying to individual perceptions" (James, 1982, p. 226). Criteria used to assess the construct validity

---

[2] For a detailed discussion of the design and testing of aggregation bias in estimates of perceptual agreement see James (1982).

of an aggregate climate score include perceptual agreement (whether a concept is applicable at both an individual and organizational level) and homogeneity of within-groups or within-organizations variance (Jones & James, 1979; Roberts et al., 1978). The validity of aggregate scores might also be determined based on the existence of a meaningful correlation between aggregate scores and other organizational level variables (Jones & James, 1979). While some dissent exists, the use of aggregated perceptual individual scores to describe the organization can be an important tool in understanding how individuals in general interpret the larger organization. However, the use of aggregated scores requires adherence to validity criteria, multiple measurement and a clearly defined research question, which indicates the appropriate unit of analysis.

Climate and Corrections Literature

While the majority of climate research is found in the industrial and organizational psychology literature, there is increasing interest in the relationship between the correctional environment and inmate and officer behavior and attitudes. Cressey (1965), with one of the earliest assessments of the importance of the 'characteristics of the organization' or climate, suggests that many of the attitudes or behaviors exhibited by inmates and officers (uncooperativeness, loyalty, honesty, aggressiveness and paranoia) are influenced or may be the result of the environment in which the individuals function. Studies of the correctional environment continue to explore this relationship. However, the growth of climate literature in corrections remains less developed than that in the areas of industrial and organizational psychology. As a result, it is necessary to address and critique the current state of climate research in corrections.

Development Of Climate Scales

As one of the earliest scholars to turn his attention to the significance of the prison environment, Moos (1968) pioneered the area of transaction-centered analysis with his incorporation of Murray's (1938) work on person/environment transactions. Moos (1975) defines his concept of organizational 'climate' as being analogous to an individual's personality or character. According to Moos (1975), climate influences an individual's "attitudes and moods, his behavior, his health and overall sense of well-being, and his social, personal and intellectual development" (p. 8). To assess this influence of climate on the individual, Moos developed the Correctional Institution Environment Scale (CIES). The scale identifies three dimensions of climate: (1) relationship, (2) personal growth and development and (3) system maintenance. These three dimensions are measured or operationalized by nine subscales: involvement, support, expressiveness, autonomy, practical orientation, personal problem orientation, order and organization, clarity and control (Wright & Goodstein, 1989).

Although used routinely for a number of years by the Federal Bureau of Prisons, the validity of the CIES has been reassessed in recent years. Criticism of the Moos CIES primarily takes four forms. First, Moos is faulted for his failure to more adequately define his concept of 'social climate' (Selo, 1976; Wright & Boudouris, 1982). Moos is also criticized for failing to account for his scale construction, neglecting to provide evidence of how he derived the three primary dimensions and nine subscales he argues represents prison climate. Third, recent research (Saylor, 1984; Wright, 1980; Wright & Boudouris, 1982) suggests there are serious problems of construct validity due to aggregation bias in cross-level inferences. Selo (1976) also addresses the issue of aggregation, criticizing Moos for "using incongruent perceptions of residents and staff as an explanatory variable...not [dealing] with the critical question of how one can compare programs when there is a lack of agreement in the perceptions of each of them" (p. 349). Finally, and perhaps most damaging, recent research indicates that, due to the high correlations among the subscales and the interrelatedness of factors, the CIES does not actually measure what it is purported to measure. Instead, two clusters are found for inmate perceptions (interpersonal and programmatic) and three dimensions for officers (operational, interpersonal and programmatic). Wright and Boudouris (1982) argue that "the relationship between suggested and derived structures is, therefore, more random than patterned, and there is no indication that the nine dimensions identified by Moos actually exist" (p. 263).

More recent developments in climate theory merge Moos's conception of climate as 'environmental presses' with Toch's (1977) emphasis on individual needs. Saylor (1984) developed the Prison Social Climate Survey which incorporates Toch's (1977) eight dimensions of environmental need (privacy, safety, structure, support, emotional feedback, social stimulation, activity and freedom). This integration of individual and environmental needs explores the relationship between individual characteristics and environmental characteristics, and the way in which these characteristics influence behavioral outcomes and attitudes. This integrated framework, which defines climate as "intervening variables which describe the conditions within an organization, as expressed in the subjective impressions of an organizational member" falls more within the conceptual framework outlined in industrial and organizational psychology literature (Saylor & Wright, 1992, p.134).

Perhaps most influential in moving the study of organizational climate forward, Saylor and Wright (1992) identify seven organizational dimensions of climate which are hypothesized to affect organizational outcomes and behavior. These seven dimensions of climate are: (1) authority and structure (how well an organization is organized and operating); (2) supervision (adequacy of supervision); (3) satisfaction (likelihood of staying with an organization; how an organization compares with others); (4) institution satisfaction (preference for working at a particular institution); (5) job satisfaction (satisfaction with particular jobs); (6) personal efficacy (influence, accomplishment and ease with which individuals experience working with inmates) and (7) job-related stress (impact of job on individual).

While this scheme appears to provide a fairly comprehensive description of the prison climate, it fails to differentiate between perceptions of the organization, its processes and procedures, and the affective responses to these structural and perceptual measures of the organization. Industrial and organizational psychology literature, clearly at the forefront of climate research, addresses the difference between perceptions of climate and affective responses to climate. However, much of corrections climate literature consistently fails to make this important distinction which unnecessarily clouds the concept of climate (e.g., Camp, 1994; Stohr et al., 1994; Whitehead & Lindquist, 1989; Wright, 1979; Wright & Saylor, 1991; Wright & Saylor, 1992).

Job satisfaction, often identified as an important variable in climate research, is one such example of an affective response. Climate generally refers to direct perceptions of the work environment. Perceptions of the job might include issues of whether an individual feels engaged in the planning or development process of work methods and procedures or if an individual feels he or she has the ability to make job related decisions. Job satisfaction, on the other hand, represents an attitudinal or an emotional evaluation of the job situation (Hershberger et al., 1994; James & Jones, 1976; Locke, 1976; Pritchard & Karasick, 1973; Rousseau, 1978; Schneider, 1975). Issues of job satisfaction include whether an individual finds the job interesting and rewarding. This type of assessment of the job situation taps into the internal state of the individual, and does not represent a descriptive analysis of the work environment. While correlated, and even reciprocally related (James & Jones, 1980), job satisfaction is a concept separate and distinct from climate. As Schneider (1975) notes:

> Job satisfaction may concern the same structural work world involved in climate research but job satisfaction implies an evaluation of structure in terms of some personal system of need or values. For climate, perceptions of practices and procedures may be organized onto a theme characterizing the organization; the organization's order is apprehended. (p. 462)

Job satisfaction refers to a worker's affective response to or evaluation of the organization, and as such is not a measure of the work environment or climate (Hershberger et al., 1994; James & Jones, 1976; Locke, 1976; Pritchard & Karasick, 1973; Rousseau, 1978; Schneider, 1975). Few researchers take exception to this conception of job satisfaction. However, one such researcher is Guion (1973), who suggests that climate is not different than job satisfaction, and that in fact both are affective responses to the organization. However, the majority of climate researchers incorporate this distinction between a descriptive and an evaluative orientation, as evidenced in their theoretical framework and modeling of causal relationships.

<u>Correctional Climate Variables.</u>

Role ambiguity has received a great deal of attention in prison climate literature, and is often referred to as role conflict. Role ambiguity has been defined as both a structural characteristic of the organization (conflicting role expectations) and an officer outcome (a feeling of conflict). As Philliber (1987) notes:

> researchers hardly seem to recognize that even individuals' role problems may take different forms...although all these role difficulties may exist for COs and for prisons, they are not the same; more careful distinction seems important. (p. 20)

For the purpose of this study, the concept that an officer perceives a work environment characterized by differing and ambiguous job demand is referred to as role ambiguity.

Role ambiguity is directly related to such officer outcomes as decreased levels of job satisfaction (Hepburn & Albonetti, 1980) and increased levels of job stress (Whitehead & Lindquist, 1986) and burnout (Manning, 1983). Interaction with overcrowding produces increase aggressiveness among officers (Jacobs & Retsky, 1975), as well as an apparent laxity in rule enforcement (Sykes, 1958). A review of the literature suggests an absence of a relationship between role ambiguity and individual-level variables.

Other indicators of climate, such as the perception of a general lack of standard policy, decision making impact, and training are associated with higher levels of job stress (Guenther & Guenther, 1974; Stalgaitis, Meyer & Krisak, 1982; Stinchcomb, 1985). The perception of a dangerous and unpredictable environment also is related to increased job stress (Guenther & Guenther, 1974; Stalgaitis et al., 1982; Stinchcomb, 1985). While a great deal of research has focused on individual-level predictors of job stress and job satisfaction, they appear for the most part to be inconsistent and weak. As such, indicators of climate appear to be better predictors of officer attitudes.

This summary of the literature focusing on several of the more salient relationships between climate variables and officer attitudes and behaviors illustrates some of the issues associated with research on social climate and correctional officers. Generally, indicators of organizational climate tend to be better predictors of outcome behavior than individual-level variables. This literature review also points to the need for more consistency in the operationalization of variables across studies in an effort to build a coherent body of knowledge.

Statement of the Problem

Jail is a coercive organization in which the use of force or its threatened use is a common occurrence. The coercive nature of the correctional institution stems from the structural position that separates the detention officer from the inmate. As Hepburn (1985) notes, "The prison guard has the right to exercise control over prisoners by virtue of the structural relationship between the position of the guard and the position of prisoner" (p.146). While the detention officer possesses government-granted authority to command, a prisoner does not necessarily feel obligated to obey (Sykes, 1958). While the method an officer relies on to maintain control or gain the compliance of inmates may vary and the actual use of force is not necessarily essential, the potential for officers to threaten or actually use force remains an underlying theme of officer/inmate interaction.[3]

The preceding review of literature has examined a number of issues regarding use of force, and although there exists a great deal of literature on use of force, nearly all of it focuses on the salient individual and situational variables associated with a police officer's use of force. The dearth of research exploring detention officers' use of force necessitates a reliance on policing literature to suggest relationships among correctional variables. Generally, it is situational variables (e.g., offender behavior, presence or absence of citizens or other officers) and not individual level variables (e.g., race, age, education, length of service) which prove to be greater predictors of use of force among police officers (Bayley & Garofalo, 1989; Friedrich, 1980;

---

[3] For a detailed discussion of the typology of bases of power and control in the prison organization, see Hepburn (1985) and Stojkovic (1986).

Hayden, 1981; Riksheim & Chermak, 1993; Sherman, 1980; Smith, 1986).

While the issue of use of force by detention officers requires further analysis, a great deal of research does address other attitudes and behaviors of correctional officers. This research generally seeks to determine the relationship among individual level variables, organizational level variables, and officers' attitudes and behaviors. Yet, such research often is conceptually fragmented and inconsistent. It fails to differentiate adequately between perceptions of the organization, its processes and procedures and affective responses to the organization. This research will benefit from being placed within the framework of climate research, which adheres to the stricter interpretation of climate developed within the industrial and organizational psychology literature.

Conceptual Definitions Utilized in this Analysis

Due to the confusion and inconsistency within the climate literature, and after a careful review of the conceptual definitions available in the industrial and organizational psychology literature, this analysis employs Pritchard and Karasick's (1973) definition of climate as:

> ...a relatively enduring quality of an organization's internal environments distinguishing it from other organizations; (a)which results from the behavior and policies of member of the organization, especially management; (b) which is perceived by members of the organization; (c) which serves as a basis for interpreting the situation; and (d) [which]

acts as a source of pressure for directing activity. (p. 127)

In keeping with Schneider's (1975) suggested terminology, 'organizational climate' is used in reference to the general area of climate research. This analysis recognizes that climate is multidimensional, with a number of climates existing within an organization (e.g., climate of structure and organization, climate of supervision).

The focus on an objective/subjective dichotomy as a means to approach the measurement of organizational properties has characterized, yet unnecessarily clouded, much of the correctional organizational climate literature (Saylor, 1984; Saylor, 1992; Saylor & Gilman, 1992). For greater clarity, this analysis instead follows the framework set out by Indik (1968), who emphasizes the need to focus first on the level of analysis and only then on the nature of the specific variable to be measured. Accordingly, this analysis builds on his framework because the focus of this analysis examines individual level perceptions of the organizational climate and how those perceptions influence a detention officer's attitudes. Dimensions of climate include structure and support, supervision, and efficacy, while affective outcomes include job satisfaction and job stress. This analysis examines the influence of these variables on a detention officer's readiness to use force.

This study employs a measurement of job satisfaction and job stress, maintaining that these variables reflect an individual's internal state by measuring an individual's affective or emotional response to the work environment and are not descriptive of the organization itself. As such, these variables are attitudinal variables and are not considered a measurement of organizational climate.

Research Questions and Hypothesis

Due to the shortcomings in both correction climate research and use of force research, the need to explore the routine exercise of force by detention officers and its relation to a variety of climates within correctional institution becomes apparent. This analysis explores the notion that the behavior and attitudes of an individual are significantly influenced by the climate within which he or she functions, and that the measurement of climate "involves a set of macro perceptions that reflect how environments are cognitively represented in terms of their psychological meaning and significance to the individual" (James, 1982, p. 219). For this reason, climate acts as a critical link between the individual and the organization. This study proposes that detention officers perceive conditions of the organizational environment, and that these perceptions, representing various climates within the institution, influence the attitudes and nature of the officers' interaction with or treatment of inmates, specifically an officer's readiness to use force.

With this in mind, it is hypothesized that measurements of climate have a direct effect on a detention officer's expressed readiness to use force. Secondly, it is hypothesized that measurements of climate have indirect effects on a detention officer's expressed readiness to use force via their effects on both job satisfaction and job stress. Finally, it is hypothesized that the observed effects of climate on an officer's expressed readiness to use force will remain statistically significant when the individual characteristics of the officer are controlled.

CHAPTER 3
The Socio-Cultural Environment

Analysis of climate occurs at the individual, group, organization and socio-cultural levels. Studies of correctional institutions at the socio-cultural or macro-level (e.g. Sykes, 1958) are essential to our understanding of the prison and jail, yet are few in number. Paraphrasing de Beaumont and de Tocqueville, Jacobs (1983) notes, "the level of a society's civilization can be judged by the state of its prisons" (p.17). However, the relationship between the socio-cultural or external climate and officers' attitudes and behavior does not receive the same attention as the other levels of analysis (Jacobs, 1983). Specific emphasis continues to be on the individual, the group and the organization which exists within the broader socio-cultural climate.

Regardless of the level of analysis used when studying the correctional organization, it is generally agreed that:

penal sanctions or institutions are not simply dependent variables at the end of some finite line of social causation. Like all social institutions, punishment interacts with its environment, forming part of the mutually constructing configuration of elements which make up the social world (Garland, 1990, p. 22).

The correctional environment is influenced by factors external to the organization itself, including social, political and economic conditions. These conditions have given rise to a series of developments which have affected correctional policy and procedure over the last thirty years, significantly impacting the role and function of the correctional institution in America. Historically, such developments included prisoners' rights movements, the trend toward the professionalization of correctional work and community-based corrections, the centralization of policy making authority, the changing nature of the inmate population (younger and more violent offenders) and sentencing reform (Blumstein, 1989; Goodstein & MacKenzie, 1989; Hepburn, 1989; Knapp, 1989).

More recent trends are of a very different nature. Since 1985, the United States has experienced a rapid increase in the population of its prisons and jails. Driving this trend is mandatory sentencing legislation, with "Congress deeming incarceration the predominant approach to deter potential offenders and incapacitate convicted criminals, especially in 'get tough' mandatory minimum sentences for repeat offenders" (Maghan, 1999, p. 200). The correctional environment also has been influenced by an increasing growth in the private prison industry, a new generation of 'super predator' inmates (see DiIulio, 1994), the growing construction of new ultrasecure 'maxi-maxi' prisons, an increasing focus on anti-prison gang policies and the continuing effects of overcrowding on correctional workforce issues (Maghan, 1999). In addition, there has been a marked change in public support for incarceration to serve the function of incapacitation and not rehabilitation. This trend toward a more punitive and retributive public attitude has resulted in an increased dehumanization of inmates, reflected in such areas as increased restrictions on prisoner recreation, a decrease in the quality of food and housing, and frequent court intervention in the management of correctional institutions.

While external developments influence the operation of the correctional organization, they also impact the individuals working within the organization. In his analysis of Stateville, Jacobs (1977) notes that just as the operation of the penitentiary was affected by changes in the external environment, many of the changes (such as racial integration and the growth of employee unionization) also greatly influenced the guards working in Stateville. Poole and Regoli (1981) argue that policy changes resulting from humanitarian reforms and the prisoners' rights movement altered officers' ability to control inmates, resulting in increased tension and fear within the correctional institution. Much like inmates, correctional officers are required to adapt and adjust to an environment that is often influenced by factors outside the correctional institution.

Maricopa County Jails

As critical as such socio-environmental factors are in influencing prison and jail policy, procedure and organization, these issues are not variables in this analysis. However, it is important to include a discussion of the unique social and political climate of this particular jail system. Maricopa County Sheriff Joe Arpaio has cultivated a national, as well as international, reputation as the "Toughest Sheriff in the Country." This reputation stems from a number of unique policies Sheriff Arpaio has implemented since being elected sheriff in 1993. These policies include efforts at making the conditions of confinement unpleasant and inhospitable, as well as the introduction of non-lethal weapons for use by all detention officers. Concern regarding his policies and practices has been raised by such human rights groups as Amnesty International, while allegations of misuse of force and inadequate health care have come under the scrutiny by the U.S. Department of Justice.

The county jail system which Sheriff Arpaio oversees is comprised of six jails and one Intake facility, with an average daily inmate population of approximately 7000 (U.S. Department of Justice, 1998). In prisoner population, the Maricopa County jail is the 7th largest jail system in the country (U.S. Bureau of Justice, 1998). It is important to note that approximately 70 percent of those being held in the Maricopa County jails are pre-trial detainees; individuals who have yet to be found guilty of any offense.

A study by Hepburn and Griffin (1998) provides some insight into the nature of this jail population. Examining four cohorts of offenders released during the first quarters 1989, 1990, 1994 and 1995 (N=4,793) it was found that a majority of offenders were convicted of offenses ranging from probation violation, traffic violations, failure to appear, contempt of court and drug-related offenses, as well as crimes against persons and property. The offenders "were sentenced to an average of 80.4 days and median of 58 days in the jail; 23.4 percent served 14 days or less and only 12.4 percent served more than six months" (Hepburn & Griffin, 1998, p.10).

Purpose of Punishment

Harsh conditions of confinement as a form of punishment can serve different purposes. One purpose of punishment is retribution. From a retributive perspective, offenders 'deserve' to be punished because they have violated the law and society has a moral obligation to sanction the individual in an effort to redress the imbalance caused by the criminal behavior. As such, the sanction imposed on the offender should be in proportion to the severity of his or her crime. A second purpose of punishment is deterrence. To achieve the goal of deterrence, a punishment must reduce the future criminal behavior of the individual being punished and/or others who witness the punishment. The severity of the punishment should be only as severe as necessary to achieve the goal of deterrence.

It is with these two publicly stated purposes, retribution and deterrence, that Sheriff Arpaio introduced a number of policies and programs that affect the conditions of confinement in the Maricopa County jails. Male and female inmates are housed separately in surplus Army tents and exposed to the extreme temperatures of Arizona's summers. Camera-equipped dogs roam the tent facilities. Male and female "chain gangs" pick up garbage on city streets, paint street curbs and help bury the indigent in the public cemetery.4 Television is restricted for large segments of the inmate population, and those who are allowed television have been limited to watching such shows as CSPAN, Disney, cooking shows, and a lecture series by Newt Gingrich. Both smoking and sexually oriented literature are prohibited for everyone. Inmates are no longer served coffee and are allowed no recreation.

---

4 Most scholars would argue that the more accurate term for the modern 'chain gang' is 'work crew'. The current practice of chaining inmates together to labor outside the prison or jail differs significantly in purpose and brutality from the practice employed in the early 1900s. The term 'chain gang' is used here as it is the name of the program operating in the Maricopa County jail system.

They are outfitted in black and white striped uniforms and pink underwear, socks and shoes. Inmates are charged a co-pay if they seek medical attention. The Sheriff is proud to note that the cost of inmate food is approximately sixty cents a day per inmate (raising questions of quality), for which inmates are charged if they have money in their jail account. More recently, the Sheriff has reduced inmate meals from three a day to two, combining breakfast with lunch.

When considering the nature of these policies, it becomes clear that Sheriff Arpaio blurs the goals of retribution and deterrence, and the way in which punishment functions to achieve these goals. As he often argues, "I don't want criminals to be happy and comfortable in my jail. So it gets hotter than hell in those tents. So what? So the baloney in the sandwiches gets a little green sometimes. So what? If you don't want to be there, don't commit the crime" (Grant, 1995, p.6). The conditions of confinement are designed to act as additional punishment to that which already is imposed by the court. As noted by Hepburn and Griffin (1998):

> According to this view, if there is some deterrent effect as a result of the idleness, boredom and deprivations of liberty which characterize detention, then policies and programs which create further deprivations and hardships should have an additional deterrent effect. In short, the general hypothesis is that the more severe the conditions of confinement experienced by the jailed offender, then the less likely is the offender to commit future crimes following release. (p. 4)

At the same time, Sheriff Arpaio makes the retributive intent of his policies clear. Regarding his concern about exposing the dogs used to patrol the tents to the high temperatures and intense heat of Arizona's summer months, Arpaio states, "I wouldn't want anything to happen to the dogs...the dogs have not committed a crime" (Sense, 1997, p. 10). Through such comments, Sheriff Arpaio suggests that since inmates have committed a crime, they are less deserving of concern regarding their conditions of confinement.

Recidivism Rates and Prisoner Responses to Jail

In response to media concerns regarding the generally harsh conditions of confinement found in Maricopa County jails, Sheriff Arpaio argues, "It is hard but humane. I'm using jail to fight crime. I want to make it so terrible that nobody will want to come back." (Steffens, 1997, p. 9). For the Sheriff and his supporters, this relationship between living conditions within the jail and the future behavior of offenders once released is clear. Inmates who are exposed to jail policies and programs which are punitive in nature and cause additional hardship will be less likely to engage in future criminal behavior to avoid being sent back to the harsh environment of the county jail. Convinced of the influence of his policies, Sheriff Arpaio commissioned a study (Hepburn & Griffin, 1998) to examine the relationship between conditions of confinement and recidivism rates. The first part of this two part study examined recidivism rates and the factors associated with the observed levels of recidivism in Maricopa County. The second part of the study explored inmate attitudes and opinions about the conditions of confinement in Maricopa County jails.

In the first phase of the study, a total of 4,793 persons who had been sentenced to the Maricopa County jail for a misdemeanor or felony offense and who were released during the first quarters of 1989, 1990, 1994 and 1995 were identified (Hepburn & Griffin, 1998). The first two cohorts represent a 'baseline', or an earlier group of inmates who were incarcerated and released prior to the implementation of Sheriff Arpaio's 'get tough' policies. The third and fourth cohorts were 'exposed' to the Sheriff's policies. In summary, the findings of this analysis indicated that there was "no systematic change, neither an increase nor a decrease, in either the type or the rate of recidivism" among released offenders between the 'baseline' group and the group 'exposed' to the Sheriff's policies (Hepburn & Griffin, 1998, p.19). Offender's age and sentence length were found to be statistically significant but modest predictors of recidivism following release. Stronger predictors of recidivism following release included offense type, number of charges at conviction, and prior arrest record. However, once these and other differences in the sample of offenders were controlled, "there was no significant difference in recidivism observed between those offenders released in 1989-1990 and those released in 1994-1995" (Hepburn & Griffin, 1998, p. 19).

The second phase of this study focused on prisoners' views of the policies and programs instituted by the Sheriff, and often unique to Maricopa County jails. As other studies have indicated (Petersilia, 1990), if policies, programs and other forms of punishment are expected to deter future criminal behavior, then the prisoners exposed to them must experience some added sense of deprivation, punishment or shame. Negative attitudes and opinions about their experience within the jail do not assure nonrecidivism, of course, but it is difficult to claim that these policies and programs are important deterrents in the absence of adverse inmate reaction. It is with this in mind that a sample of persons sentenced to the jail was interviewed immediately prior to release. Two hundred and twenty-six inmates were asked a series of questions regarding their likelihood of returning to jail, as well as specific jail policies and general conditions of confinement.

About one-third of inmates interviewed indicated there was some likelihood they would be back, many citing such reasons as no change in life style or circumstances that resulted in their detention (e.g., continued use of alcohol or drugs, inability to pay fines or child support, or a need to drive to work even though one's license is suspended). Others emphatically stated that there was little or no possibility that they would return to jail or prison. When asked why, many said that they had 'learned their lesson' and would not make similar mistakes again. For a large number of prisoners, especially those who served short sentences, many of the policies and programs were irrelevant. Many inmates do not seek medical attention while detained, and very few inmates actually work on the chain gang. Prisoners who are sentenced to one or two days detention are not issued striped uniforms and pink underwear and they are not assigned to jobs.

The policies or programs that adversely affected the most inmates were those that applied to all inmates. The most problematical were the policies of one cold meal a day, the lack of recreation, the prohibition of smoking and the absence of coffee. Surprisingly, the programs and policies that elicit the most publicity and are often viewed as the most controversial (chain gangs, striped uniforms and pink underwear) generally receive the least attention or concern from the inmates interviewed. For example, many prisoners view the chain gang as a publicity stunt and few are opposed to it. "Many see the chain gangs as an emotional and physical outlet – especially in the absence of recreation – that helps pass the time, controls tempers, and builds self-esteem" (Hepburn & Griffin, 1998, p. 28).

The issuance of pink underwear and striped uniforms received little complaint among those interviewed. "Comments from prisoners ranged from those who saw the policy as "silly" or "amusing" and whose only concern was whether or not the clothing was clean and comfortable to those who believed the practice was "degrading" and "depressing" (Hepburn & Griffin, 1998, p. 31). Most saw the policy as irrelevant. Being housed in Army surplus tents received mixed reviews. Many inmates preferred the tents to being confined in a small, warm and stuffy cell. At the same time, however, prisoners complained about the heat during the summer and problems with mice, ants and scorpions.

Apparently, what affects most inmates and what most affects the inmates are those conditions of confinement that determine the level of their physical comfort while detained: the food, the temperature, the absence of exercise, and the adjustments necessary to coexist in close quarters with so many strangers. In general, the study found that the policies put into place by Sheriff Arpaio tended not to evoke the kind of strong, negative reaction necessary to raise the level of deterrence beyond that which comes as a result of incarceration.

Non-lethal Weapons into the County Jail

In addition to the unique conditions of confinement existing within the Maricopa County jails, it is important to note other developments which have the potential to influence the jail climate, as well as the study at hand. In general, the availability of non-lethal weapons (stun device and pepper spray) in the jail setting is not standard policy. A survey by the Institute for Law and Justice (1993) of 154 jails found that only about half the jails made chemical irritants and batons available for use by security staff. A stun device was available in approximately one third of the jails. In addition, although the weapons were 'available', they were not standard issue for all security staff. Quite often, non-lethal weapons are stored in a central arsenal or are distributed only to supervisory staff.

Data for this research project were collected in conjunction with an evaluation sponsored by the National Institute of Justice (NIJ) and the National Sheriffs' Association (NSA) regarding the introduction of non-lethal weapons into the Maricopa County Jails. In 1994, non-lethal weapons were introduced into the six jails and Intake center operated by the Maricopa County Sheriff's Office. The National Institute of Justice and the National Sheriff's Association supplied the Sheriff's Office with enough handheld stun devices and pepper spray canisters to arm every detention officer. They also funded the requisite module of pre-service and in-service training for each officer prior to the distribution of the weapons.

The use of force policy implemented in conjunction with the non-lethal weapons was "designed to reduce physical contact with the inmate, thereby reducing the possibility that the inmate and/or officer might be injured in a scuffle or fight in an environment of steel furniture bolted to concrete walls and floors" (Hepburn et al., 1997, p. 4). According to Arpaio (1994), "when suspects or jail inmates refuse to respond peacefully to lawful instructions, the pepperspray or stun device certainly is more efficient and humane then heavy physical force" (p. 3). The policy, which placed the use of non-lethal weapons before the use of 'hands-on' tactics on the use of force continuum, was soon revised. In response to officers' initial reluctance to use these weapons, the policy was rewritten so that both the weapons and 'hands-on' tactics were equivalent responses on the use of force continuum. In August 1995, after receiving notice that the U.S. Department of Justice was investigating the jail system and in response to external experts visiting the jails, the policy was revised again, elevating the non-lethal weapons just above the use of 'hands-on' tactics.

In addition to the officer training and the distribution of the pepper spray and stun device, the grant required an evaluation component. Evaluative data were collected through an Altercation reporting form completed by the principal officer involved in any use of force incident and co-signed by his or her supervising officer. A survey of all officers was conducted prior to, during and after the introduction of the non-lethal weapons, and information regarding staff and inmate injuries was collected as well. This evaluation provides insight not only into officer attitudes toward the non-lethal weapons and the effectiveness of non-lethal weapons, but also into instances of when force was threatened or actually used by officers against inmates in Maricopa County jails.

The introduction of the nonlethal weapons was not readily accepted by either supervisory officers or detention officers. Having been trained in both 'soft' and 'hard' hand-on techniques, officers felt uncomfortable with the new weapons and questioned their utility. Officers expressed concerns that inmates may take the weapons and use them against officers. With training and practice, however, resistance to the weapons faded. By 1996, "when all officers had been trained with the weapons and had been armed with the weapons for at least a year, there was a consensus among officers that the weapons play a useful role in their facilities" (Hepburn et al., 1997, p.9). For those officers who had used the weapons, seventy to ninety percent agreed with the statements that nonlethal weapons affect inmate misconduct, make inmates easier to control and reduce injuries to officers and inmates (Hepburn et al., 1997).

A second measure of acceptance is the extent to which officers used the stun device and pepperspray. The study indicated that "there was a steady increase over time in both the monthly frequency of nonlethal weapon use and the proportion of all incidents in which nonlethal weapons were used rather than hands-on tactics" (Hepburn et al., 1997, p.18). During the two year period of the study, there were a total of 2,995 reported incidents in which a detention officer or supervisor used force. A total of 3,250 inmates were involved in these altercations with officers. In general, the stun device was used more often than the pepperspray, and in those situations in which a nonlethal weapon was used, the weapon was "more likely to be actually used, or applied, rather than simply displayed or threatened" (Hepburn et al., 1997, p.23).

Interestingly enough, when exploring the effect the nonlethal weapons had on aspects of the jail environment, "there was no observed change over time in either of the two factors which would appear to be most affected by the introduction of nonlethal weapons – fear of attack [by inmates] or authority over inmates" (Hepburn et al., 1997, p.42). Those areas in which the introduction of the weapons produce some measurable effects over time included an increase in officers' job satisfaction and commitment to the Sheriff's office and a decrease in job stress.

Concerns Regarding Conditions of Confinement

These policies, and the general climate to which they contribute, have come under attack by a number of agencies concerned over reports of abuse and violations of human rights. The United States Justice Department conducted an investigation in late 1995 in response to concerns regarding excessive use of force, as well as denial of adequate medical care. After their investigation, the U.S. Dept. of Justice concluded that "unconstitutional conditions existed at the jails with respect to (1) the use of excessive force against inmates and (2) the deliberate indifference to inmates serious medical needs" (Deval, 1996, p.1). More specifically, the Justice Department found excessive force in use at three facilities, including the application of force to prisoners without any initial justification (i.e., to hasten movement, to send a message); the application of more force than necessary to accomplish a legitimate goal (i.e. kicking in head, punching, shoving to gain control of an inmate); the application of force even after an inmate is completely restrained (i.e. using stun guns when inmate is cuffed or in restraint chair); and the use of hog-tying inmates as a form of restraint (Deval, 1996).

Interestingly enough, the expert employed by the Department of Justice noted that he was "frankly amazed to discover that virtually every detention officer whom [he]observed throughout the entire jail system was carrying non-lethal weapons on his or her person" (Deval, 1996, p.

4). As discussed earlier, it was the National Institute of Justice, the research division of the U.S. Department of Justice, which funded the project to introduce non-lethal weapons into this county jail. In addition to this "overavailability of non-lethal weapons," the Justice Department reported that the use of excessive force at the jails was "facilitated by several interrelated systemic factors" including inadequate staffing levels, youthfulness and inexperience of jail staff, overcrowding in the intake processing center, insufficient inservice training, and inadequate use of force reports, use of force investigations, and tracking of potentially problematic staff (Deval, 1996, p. 4). Since this investigation was completed, the Maricopa County Sheriff's Office has worked with the U.S. Department of Justice to address the issues raised in their report, making improvements in medical care and conditions of confinement.

In June of 1997, Amnesty International sent a delegation to the Maricopa County Jail to collect information regarding the conditions of confinement. This organization, like the U.S. Department of Justice, expressed concern over the conditions of the jail facilities and the excessive use of force by detention officers. In particular, Amnesty International's concern stemmed from the Justice Department's findings, as well as the highly publicized death of an inmate while in custody of the Sheriff's office. Amnesty International met with jail officials and inmates' attorneys, toured the main intake unit and the tent facility, and reviewed several cases where the use of force appeared unwarranted. According to Amnesty International (1997), the force alleged in these and other cases appears to have been excessive and to have amounted to cruel, inhuman or degrading treatment in violation of the USA's obligations under international human rights standards and treaties" (p. 4) More specifically, Amnesty International came out against the use of stun devices, the use of a restraint chair, the lack of adequate physical exercise, the housing of inmates in the Tents facility and use of chain gangs. Although Sheriff Arpaio did respond to the criticisms raised in the government's report, it is important to note few changes were made to the policies outlined earlier, including the use of tent housing facilities, the availability of non-lethal weapons and the use of the restraint chair and chain gang.

Conclusion

The Maricopa County jail system is a unique one, both in terms of the policies implemented by the county's sheriff and the extent of media exposure. Many of the policies have been introduced as cost-saving programs (tent facilities, two meals a day), while others as means to punish and deter. Regarding the use of force in this jail system, it is important to remember that the nonlethal weapons were introduced for legitimate and even humane purposes to maintain control and to reduce injuries to inmates and officers. It appears that the nonlethal weapons may have indeed had that effect. However, the presence of these weapons, together with a public rhetoric which demonizes and devalues inmates, and with a number of polices and practices which further deprive and humiliate inmates, creates a climate of repression. This is a climate that is produced by the organization itself, but it also is formed and molded by public perception, intense media coverage and government intervention. The extent to which such a climate influences a detention officer's attitudes toward the use of force is unknown. One would have to guess, however, that officers' attitudes toward inmates are more likely than not affected by such policies and rhetoric, and that such a climate does not serve to enhance interactions between officers and inmates.

CHAPTER 4
Methodology

Subjects and Procedures

All detention officers working in the seven jails of Maricopa County, Arizona, received a self-administered survey in July 1996. With the assistance and support of the administration, the questionnaires and a cover letter of introduction were distributed by shift supervisors and each officer was asked to return the anonymous survey to the shift supervisor in an unmarked envelope (See Appendix A for cover letter).[5]   Response rates varied between 65 percent and 100 percent among the seven jails. Of the 72 officers surveyed, 617 (79.9%) returned a usable questionnaire, which became the basis for this analysis.[6]

---

[5] These data were collected in conjunction with an evaluation sponsored by the National Institute of Justice and the National Sheriffs' Association regarding the introduction of non-lethal weapons into the Maricopa County Jails. As such, this researcher had the assistance and support of the Maricopa County Jail administration when collecting the data on which this analysis is based.

[6] Although the use of shift supervisors to distribute and collect officer surveys raises an issue of bias, this researcher believes that the

A Note on Samples Versus Populations

It is important to note that all detention officers working within the seven Maricopa County Jails were surveyed. Consequently, these data represent the population of detention officers in Maricopa County and not a sample of that population. The use of tests of statistical significance on associations observed in such data is a common practice, but it is highly problematic. As Babbie (1995) notes, "tests of statistical significance measure the likelihood of relationships between variables being only a product of sampling error; if there's no sampling, there's no error" (p. 440). As such, statistical tests of probability are not strictly legitimate. However, this research attempts to test various hypotheses regarding the relationship between individual level factors, organizational climate and an officer's perceived readiness to use force, and widely understood significance levels serve as useful criteria for assessing these relationships. Although failing to meet assumptions of a sampling design, the use of significance tests provides this researcher with what Babbie (1995) refers to as "data-dredging techniques," yet at the same time the use of significance tests limits one's ability for strict statistical interpretation (p. 440).

---

accompanying cover letter addressing issues of confidentiality, the well established relationship between the officers and evaluators, as well as the manner in which the surveys were returned (many not filled out or unusable), negates the potential complication of this issue. In addition, while items from this survey serve as the basis for this study on the potentially sensitive subject of use of force, the survey, when taken as a whole, does not focus primarily on the issue of force.

Obviously, the more important issue is one of substantive significance. With such a large number of cases, any association among variables, regardless of how small, becomes significant. Great caution must be used to differentiate between statistical and substantive significance.

Organizational Climate Scales

In this study, individual level perceptions of the organizational situation are measured. The multidimensional concept of climate is comprised of three areas of interest:

(1)   structure and organization (the way in which the institution is organized and operating),
(2)   supervision and support (leadership and support from both supervisors and the larger institution), and
(3)   personal efficacy (influence and ease with which individuals experience working with inmates).

The development of these areas of interest, within which specific measurements of climate are contained, is informed by Saylor and Wright's (1992) seven dimensions of climate, as well as James and Jones's (1976) conception of climate, wherein climate represents perceptions of "characteristics of the job, the leadership, the workgroup and the various subsystems as well as the total organization" (p. 100). Several indicators within each dimension are possible, and this study relies on Likert-like scales to operationalize multiple indicators. These dimensions incorporate scales reflecting officer perceptions of the organizational environment in which they work

Structure and organization

There are three indicators of institutional structure and organization. One is the eight-item institutional and organizational operations scale previously used by Saylor (1992) to measure each officer's perception of the daily operations of the facility. The eight statements to which the officers responded are:

(1)   The information I get through formal communication channels helps me to perform my job effectively.
(2)   In this jail, it is often unclear who has formal authority to make a decision.
(3)   It's really not possible to change things here.
(4)   I am told promptly when there is a change in policy, rules, or regulations that affect me.
(5)   I have the authority I need to accomplish my work objectives.
(6)   Employees do not have much opportunity to influence what goes on here.
(7)   Under the present system, promotions are seldom related to employee performance.
(8)   Management is flexible enough to make changes when necessary.

As summarized in Table 1, the item-to-item coefficients of this scale range from .20 to .53 and the scale has a reliability coefficient of .82. The responses` to these eight items are coded such that the greater the numeric score, the more favorable the officer's assessment of institutional and organizational operations.

A second scale measures an officer's perception of the *training* received as a detention officer. This five-item scale (alpha = .85), based on one previously developed by Logan (1993) and is comprised of the following statements:

(1)   I receive the kind of training from MCSO that I need to perform my work well.

(2)   MCSO training has improved my job skills.

(3)   The supervisors support the MCSO training staff.

(4)   My MCSO training has helped me to work effectively with inmates.

(5)   The MCSO training program did not prepare me to deal with situations that arise on the job.

Finally, *role ambiguity* is operationalized by an eight-item scale which measures the extent to which an officer perceives differing and ambiguous job demands. Based on role ambiguity scales previously used by Hepburn and Albonetti (1980), Poole and Regoli (1980a), Hepburn (1985) and Hepburn and Knepper (1993), this scale has a reliability coefficient of .86.

(1)   Often times, one rule will tell us to do one thing, but another rule tells us to do something else.

(2)   One of the problems here is that it's never very clear as to who is responsible for doing different jobs.

(3)   There are so many people telling us what to do here that you never can be sure who the real boss is.

(4)   When a problem comes up here, the staff seldom agrees on how it should be handled.

(5)   If I followed all the rules, my job would never get done.

(6)   The rules and regulations are clear enough here that I know specifically what I can and cannot do on my job.

(7)   The rules I am supposed to follow here never seem to be very clear.

(8)   There are so many rules and regulations telling me how to do my job that I am not sure I can follow all of them.

Supervision and support

This study relies on two measures of supervision and support. First, a five-item scale measures the officer's perception of the *quality of supervision* received within the facility (Saylor, 1984). It has a reliability coefficient of .83.

The five items used are:

(1)   My supervisor engages me in the planning process, such as developing work methods and procedures for my job.

(2)   My supervisor gives me adequate information on how well I am performing.

(3)   I often receive feedback from my supervisor for good performance.

(4)   On my job, I know what my supervisor expects of me.

(5)   My supervisor asks my opinion when a work-related problem arises.

A second scale measures each officer's perception of *the* degree of *organizational support* received from the Maricopa County Sheriff's Office (MCSO). This four-item scale (alpha = .84), is based on a scale previously used by Eisenberger et al. (1986).

The items which comprise this scale are:
(1)   MCSO shows that it appreciates extra effort from me.
(2)   If given the chance, MCSO would take advantage of me.
(3)   Even if I did the best possible job, MCSO probably wouldn't notice.
(4)   MCSO shows it is concerned about me personally.

Personal efficacy

Three scales operationalize personal efficacy. The first scale, with an reliability coefficient of .63 measures an officer's perception of his or her own *authority* within the jail setting. This two-item scale, previously used by Hepburn and Crepin (1984) and Hepburn and Knepper (1993), is based on responses to the following statements:

(1)   I feel I have more than enough power to keep inmates in line around here.
(2)   Changes and reforms are weakening the officer's authority over inmates.

The responses to these items are coded such that the greater the numeric score, the higher the level of perceive authority.

A second scale measures the level of *alienation* that an officer experiences at work. This five-item scale has a reliability coefficient of .77. The scale is based on one previously used by Toch and Klofas (1982), and is formed with the following statement:

(1) As officers, we are damned if we do and damned if we don't.

(2) I don't have an opportunity to exercise my own judgment in doing my job.

(3) No one ever asks an officer for suggestions related to the job.

(4) If it's an officer's word against an inmate, they'll believe the inmate.

(5) An officer is told what his/her job is only when he does something wrong.

Finally, a third scale measures fear of victimization, or an officer's perception of potential victimization (alpha=.70). This is a four-item scale, previously used by Hepburn and Crepin (1984):

(1) One of the worst things about being an officer here is that you never know when an inmate might try to really hurt you.

(2) The chances of getting hurt while you are working here are pretty good.

(3) I feel safe when working among inmates here.

(4)   I worry a lot about getting attacked by inmates.

Mediating Affective Scales

Job satisfaction and job stress represent two widely studied attitudes or affective responses to the organizational climate. Likert-like scales are used to measure the level of job satisfaction and job stress with which detention officers respond to the organizational situation.

<u>Job satisfaction.</u>

The general level of *job satisfaction* experienced by the respondents is measured by a six-item scale (see Hepburn, 1985; Hepburn & Albonetti, 1980; Saylor, 1992). The six statements are:

(1)   I like the duties I perform in my job.
(2)   I am satisfied with my present job assignment.
(3)   I enjoy most of the work I do here.
(4)   My job suits me very well.
(5)   If I had the chance, I would get a job in something other than what I am doing now.
(6)   My job is usually worthwhile.

The alpha reliability coefficient for this scale is .86.

<u>Job-related stress.</u>

One Likert-like scale is used to operationalize this affective response to climate. The four-item scale (alpha =

.71) measures the level of *stress* experienced by an officer at work (Cullen, Link, Wolfe & Frank, 1985). These items are:

(1)   Usually I am calm and at ease on the job.
(2)   I usually feel that I am under a lot of pressure when I am at work.
(3)   A lot of the time, my job makes me very angry.
(4)   There are a lot of things about my job which can make me pretty upset.

Dependent Variable

Readiness to use force scale

The dependent variable, *Readiness to Use Force*, is measured by a six-item Likert-like scale. Because no similar measure existed, nine items were developed for possible use in the evaluation report. These items were designed to reflect current training issues and jail policy. Once administered, a scale (alpha = .65) was created on the basis of responses to these six statements:

(1)   If an inmate refuses to obey after the third direct command, an officer who doesn't use force is only asking for future troubles with inmates.
(2)   When a situation calls for the use of force, it would be a sign of weakness not to use force.

(3)   To minimize trouble with inmates, it's better for the officer to be aggressive and take charge of the situation.

(4)   An officer who does not use force when it is called for will have to explain himself to others.

(5)   It's to an officer's advantage to use force whenever it's justified because it sends a message to the inmates.

(6)   When in doubt, it's almost always better to use force to get results rather than just keep talking to an inmate.

Data Analysis

In light of the fact that all operationalizations are interval level data and given the rather normal distribution of the dependent variable, this analysis employs multivariate analysis, relying on Ordinary Least Squares regression models.

As such, this analysis takes advantage of the power and robustness of OLS regression to test the effects of these measures of climate on a detention officer's expressed readiness to use force. The simultaneous inclusion of all variables into the equation permits an examination of the independent and additive direct and indirect effects of the measures of climate on readiness to use force. Individual attributes such as race, gender, age, education and tenure of employment are included in this model and treated as exogenous variables to control for their effects.

Table 1 presents the descriptive statistics for the variables included in this study. As noted in Table 1, approximately three-fourths of the officers surveyed are male. For the analysis, race is dichotomized into non-white (0) and white (1), with only fifteen percent of the detention officers being persons of color. Detention officers have a mean age of 35 years and a mean education level of 13.5 years. Tenure of employment is measured by the number of months employed by the Maricopa County Sheriff's Office, with officers having been employed an average of 72.2 months, or 6 years.

Table 1 also presents descriptive statistics relating to the eleven scales representing measurements of climate, affective factors and the dependent variable, Readiness to Use Force.

Table 1
Descriptive Statistics for Variables Included in Models

Variable	Coding	N	Percentage	X̄	SD
Individual Characteristics					
Gender	1=Male	452	74.1		
	0=Female	158	25.9		
Race	1=White	511	84.6		
	0=Not White	93	15.4		
Age				36.1	11.1
Education				13.5	1.6
Tenure (months employed)				72.2	59.3

Variable	# of Items	Value Range	X̄	SD	Range of Inter-Item Correlation Coefficient	Alpha Reliability Coefficient
Climate Variables						
Alienation	5	5-25	14.2	4.3	.33 - .50	.77
Authority	2	2-10	5.4	1.9	.46	.63
Fear of Victimization	4	4-20	12.2	3.2	.31 - .47	.70
Institutional Operations	8	8-40	25.11 5.4	6.3	.20 - .53	.82
Organizational Support	4	4-20	10.2	3.9	.48 - .66	.84
Quality of Supervision	5	5-25	15.3	4.6	.39 - .70	.83
Role of Ambiguity	8	8.40	20.9	6.4	.34 - .59	.86
Training	5	5.25	16.8	4.2	.30 - .72	.85
Affective Variables						
Job Satisfaction	6	6-30	22.2	4.8	.41 - .64	.86
Job Stress	4	4-20	9.9	3.1	.26 - .55	.71
Dependent Variable						
Readiness to Use Force	6	6-30	17.2	4.2	.08 - .41	.65

CHAPTER 5
Data Analysis and Results

Bivariate Analysis

Individual Level Variables

Table 2 presents the bivariate coefficients among all the variables in the model. Consistent with previous research, gender and education level are not significantly associated with any climate variable included in this analysis. However, gender is found to have a significant although weak association with readiness to use force (.11). Race is found to be significantly associated only with fear of victimization (-.15). Age has a significant but weak association with authority (.14), training (-.09), and readiness to use force (-.17). Finally, tenure is significantly associated with five of the seven climate variables (authority, .10; fear of victimization, -.09; institutional operations, -.17; organizational support, -.15; quality of supervision, -.09; and training, -.21), as well as with the affective variable, job stress (.12). Tenure also is significantly related to readiness to use force (-.14).

Climate Variables

Stronger correlations occur among climate variables. Authority is highly correlated with all other work environment variables. Officers reporting higher levels of authority also report higher levels of organizational support, institutional operations, organizational support, quality of supervision and training and lower levels of fear of victimization and role ambiguity. Similarly, institutional operations is strongly and positively associated with organizational support (.66), quality of supervision (.64) and training (.59), and negatively associated with alienation (.74), fear of victimization (-.14) and role ambiguity (-.76). Organizational support and quality of supervision exhibit a similar relationship among climate variables. Alienation, fear of victimization and role ambiguity, on the other hand, are negatively correlated with all other climate variables and positively correlated with each other.

Affective Mediating Variables

Each climate variable displays a moderate to strong correlation with job satisfaction and job stress. A strong negative relationship exists between job satisfaction and alienation (-.44), as well as between job satisfaction and role ambiguity (-.47). A weaker, negative relationship exists between job satisfaction and fear of victimization (-.12). Higher levels of job satisfaction are significantly related to higher levels of authority (.26), institutional operations (.54), organizational support (.42), quality of supervision (.46) and training (.42).

The exact opposite relationship exists between job stress and all climate variables. A strong positive relationship exists between job stress and alienation (.45), as well as between job stress and role ambiguity (.56). Job stress also has a positive, though more moderate, relationship with fear of victimization (.30). High levels of job stress are correlated with lower levels of authority (-.35), institutional operations (-.53), organizational support (-.37), quality of supervision (-.34) and training (-.31).

Readiness to Use Force

The main variable of interest, readiness to use force, is moderately associated with job satisfaction (-.11) and job stress (.23). Officers who express lower levels of job satisfaction and higher levels of job stress also show a greater readiness to use force. All climate variables except training and quality of supervision also are significantly correlated with an officer's readiness to use force. Authority has a strong negative correlation (-.39) with readiness to use force. Institutional operations and organizational support also exhibit a negative, though more moderate, relationship with readiness to use force (-.10 and -.11, respectively). Higher levels of alienation, fear of victimization and role ambiguity are associated with higher levels of readiness to use force. As hypothesized, an officer's readiness to use force is only slightly correlated with individual level variables such as gender (.11), age (-.17) and tenure (-.14). Interestingly, readiness to use force does not vary significantly by either race or education of the officer.

Table 2

Correlation Matrix (Pearson's r) For Variables Included in Multivariate Analysis

	1	2	3	4	5	6	7	8	9	10	11	12	13	14	15	16
1 Male	1.0															
2 White	.12	1.0														
3 Age	-05	.04	1.0													
4 Educate	.04	-.06	.14[a]	1.0												
5 Tenure	-07	.02	.60[a]	.03	1.0											
6 Alien	-06	-.02	-08	-.01	-05	1.0										
7 Author	-06	.05	.14[a]	-.03	.10[b]	-.55[a]	1.0									
8 Victim	.06	-.15[a]	-.07	.01	-.09[b]	.26[a]	-.37[a]	1.0								
9 Inst Oper	.07	.02	-.08	-.00	-.17[a]	.74[a]	.47[a]	-.14[a]	1.0							
10 Org Support	.04	-.02	-.02	-.03	-.15[a]	-.60[a]	.37[a]	-.17[a]	.66[a]	1.0						
11 Qual Super	.07	.02	-.08	-.03	-.09[b]	-.61[a]	.26[a]	-.07	.64[a]	.54[a]	1.0					
12 Role Ambg	-06	-.04	-.01	.02	-.06	.74[a]	-.50[a]	.22[a]	-.76[a]	-.55[a]	-.55[a]	1.0				
13 Training	.06	-.01	-.09[b]	-.06	-.21[a]	-.48[a]	.23[a]	-.08[b]	.59[a]	.49[a]	.47[a]	.56[a]	1.0			
14 Job Satisfac	-05	.08	.07	-.04	.00	-.44[a]	.26[a]	-.12[a]	.54[a]	.42[a]	.46[a]	.47[a]	.42[a]	1.0		
15 Job Stress	-04	-.05	.05	-.08	.12[a]	.45[a]	-.35[a]	.30[a]	-.53[a]	-.37[a]	-.34[a]	.56[a]	-.31[a]	-.50[a]	1.0	
16 Use of Force	.11	.05	-.17[a]	-.04	-.14[a]	-.19[a]	-.39[a]	.28[a]	-.10[b]	-.11[a]	.02	.20[a]	-.01	-.11[a]	-.23[a]	1.0

[a]p<.01 [b]p<.05

Summary

It is interesting to note that while significant relationships exist between some individual level variables and climate, as well as individual level variables and readiness to use force, such relationships are neither numerous nor strong. As hypothesized, stronger correlations exist between climate variables and readiness to use force. While these bivariate results are interesting, they are not conclusive. To more completely understand the relationship between climate and force, it is important to use multivariate models which will identify the independent effects of each factor on force while simultaneously controlling statistically for the effects of the other factors entered into the model.

Multivariate Analysis

Regression of Readiness to Use Force on Climate and Individual Level Variables

Table 3 presents results from two models assessing the influence of climate variables and individual level variables on an officer's readiness to use force. The first model incorporates only climate variables, while the second model assesses the influence of both climate variables and individual level variables on an officer's readiness to use force. The first model regresses readiness to use force on the eight climate variables simultaneously. The combined effect of these eight variables is significant, with an adjusted R^2 of .19. Although the linear and additive effects of the eight climate variables have a statistically significantly influence an officer's readiness to use force, authority, fear of victimization, quality of supervision and role ambiguity are the only climate variables to have a statistically significant direct effect on readiness to use force. Authority has the strongest direct effect on an officer's readiness to use force (-.33), indicating that officers who feel they have higher levels of authority are less ready to use force against inmates. While exerting a direct positive effect on an officer's readiness to use force, fear of victimization, quality of supervision and role ambiguity are less of a predictor of an officer's readiness to use force than is authority. Alienation, institutional operations, organizational support and training all fail to have a statistically significant direct effect on a detention officer's readiness to use force.

The regression of readiness to use force on climate variables and individual level variables also is presented in Table 3. As hypothesized, individual level variables are not statistically significant predictors of an officer's readiness to use force. When entered into the regression model with the eight measurements of climate, gender, race, age education and tenure do little to explain the variance in an officer's readiness to use force. This supports previous research indicating that the climate in which officers operate is a much better, but still only moderate, predictor of officers' attitudes and behaviors than individual-level factors (Whitehead & Lindquist, 1989). While the overall model remains significant, the amount of variance explained does not change. In addition, none of the individual level variables exert a significant direct effect on readiness to use force. However, the addition of the socio-demographic variables does alter slightly the influence of the climate variables. Role ambiguity no longer directly affects an officer's readiness to use force and the standardized beta weights of the remaining significant climate variables change. Although decreasing slightly, the perception of the authority one exercises continues to be the strongest predictor of an officer's readiness to use force (-.29). The influence of fear of victimization and quality of supervision on an officer's readiness to use force increases slightly, from .13 to .15 and .17 to .20, respectively. While exerting some influence on the climate variables entered into this model, the inclusion of individual level variables in the regression equation fails to further explain the variance in a detention officer's readiness to use force.

There appears to be some indication of support for the major hypothesis in that climate factors affect force, and continue to do so when individual factors are controlled. However, it is important to note that only some of the climate factors have a statistically significantly affect force. Authority, fear of victimization and quality of supervision have a statistically significant direct effect on readiness to use force, while alienation, institutional operations, organizational support, role ambiguity and training do not.

Regression of Climate on Individual Level Variables

The regression of each of the eight measures of climate on individual level variables is presented in Table 4. Individual level variables explain little or no variance in a detention officer's perception of various climates within the correctional institution. Models measuring the linear and additive effects of gender, race, age, education and tenure on an officer's perception of alienation, authority, quality of supervision and role ambiguity did not yield a significant F ratio. Those models measuring the linear and additive effects of gender, race, age, education and tenure on perceptions of fear of victimization, institutional operations, organizational support and training are significant. When fear of victimization is regressed on all individual level variables, only race proves to have a significant direct effect. Minority officers express higher levels of fear of victimization than non-minority officers. However, the model as a whole explains only 2% of the variance in an officer's fear of victimization. However, each model explains only a small proportion of the total variance, ranging from 2% to 5% (see Table 4). While having a statistically significant influence on fear of victimization, race does not directly influence any other climate variable included in this analysis.

Although the linear and additive effects of individual level variables have a statistically significant influence an officer's perception of institutional operations, only tenure has a direct effect. Tenure has a statistically significant negative effect on an officer's perception of institutional operations. The inclusion of the five individual level variables in this model explains only 3% of the variance in an officer's perception of institutional operations.

Tenure also has a significant direct effect on an officer's perception of organizational support. The longer the detention officer has worked as an MCSO detention officer, the lower the level of perceived support from the organization. Although not as strong and in the opposite direction, age also has a significant direct effect on perceptions of organizational support. Older officers perceive higher levels of organizational support than younger officers. While age and tenure have a direct effect on organizational support, the model as a whole accounts for only 3% of the explained variance.

Once again, tenure proves to have a statistically significant direct effect on climate. Tenure significantly influences an officer's perception of the adequacy of training. As with institutional operations and organizational support, tenure negatively influences an officer's perceptions of training. Those officers employed by MCSO for a longer period of time perceive training as less adequate than those officers employed for shorter periods of time.

In summary, gender and education fail to explain any of the variance of the eight measures of climate. Age significantly affects only officer perception of organizational support, while race significantly influences only fear of victimization. Perhaps it is appropriate that the only factor to show systematic effect on measures of climate is tenure, since tenure represents the length of time exposed to that climate.

Table 3

Regression Analysis Summary Table for Regression of Use of Force on Climate Variables and Individual Level Variables

	Readiness to Use Force			
	(1)		(2)	
	B	SE	B	SE
Climate Variables				
Alienation	.06	.07	.04	.08
Authority	-.33[a]	.11	-.29[a]	.12
Fear of Victimization	-.13[a]	.06	-.15[a]	.06
Institutional Operations	.13	.05	.06	.05
Organizational Support	-.04	.06	-.06	.06
Quality of Supervision	.17[a]	.05	.20[a]	.05
Role Ambiguity	.16[b]	.04	.08	.05
Training	.05	.05	-.01	.05
Individual Level Variables				
Male	-----		.07	.41
White	-----		.04	.52
Age	-----		-.08	.02
Education	-----		-.06	.11
Tenure	-----		-.05	.00
Adjusted R^2	.19		.19	
F Ratio	17.08[a]		9.88[a]	

[a]$p < .01$ [b]$p < .05$

Table 4

Regression Analysis Summary Table for Regression of Climate Variables on Individual Level Variables

	Alienation		Authority		Fear of Victimization		Institutional Operations		Organizational Support		Quality of Supervision		Role Ambiguity		Training	
	B	SE	B	SE	B	SE	B	SE	B	SE	B	SE	B	SE	B	SE
Individual Level Variables																
Male	-.07	.43	-.02	.19	.07	.32	.05	.62	.03	.39	.06	.46	-.06	.65	.04	.42
White	-.01	.52	.02	.23	-.14[a]	.38	-.00	.78	-.03	.47	.01	.56	-.03	.79	-.02	.50
Age	-.08	.02	.12	.01	-.02	.02	.03	.03	.14[b]	.02	-.04	.02	-.07	.03	.08	.02
Education	-.03	.12	-.02	.05	-.01	.09	.01	.17	-.04	.11	-.00	.13	.02	.18	-.06	.12
Tenure	-.02	.00	.03	.00	-.08	.00	-.21[a]	.01	-.23[a]	.00	-.06	.00	.10	.01	-.27[a]	.00
Adjusted R^2	.01		.01		.02		.03		.03		.00		.00		.05	
F Ratio	1.50		2.10		3.50[a]		4.41[a]		3.88[a]		1.42		1.32		6.66[a]	

[a] $p < .01$ [b] $p < .05$

Regression of Job Satisfaction and Job Stress on Climate
and Individual Level Variables

Models estimating the influence of climate and socio-
demographic variables on job satisfaction and job stress are
presented in Table 5. The first model represents the
regression of job satisfaction on only the climate variables.
In the second model, individual level variables also are
entered into stress on all climate variables only. Finally,
the fourth model regresses job stress on both climate and
individual level variables.

The first model, regressing job satisfaction on all
climate variables, is significant and explains a moderate
proportion of variance (33 percent) in job satisfaction. Job
satisfaction is statistically significantly affected by three
climate variables. Institutional operations, quality of
supervision and training exert a statistically significant
positive effect on job satisfaction. A cursory review of the
regression coefficients reveals that institutional operations
has a greater influence on job satisfaction than either
quality of supervision or training.

The second equation represents the regression of job
satisfaction on both the climate and the individual level
variables simultaneously. This model also is statistically
significant, with a slightly greater proportion of variance
explained (34 percent). When both sets of variables are
entered into the equation, the three climate variables found
to be significant in the first equation remain statistically
significant and no other climate variables emerge as
significant predictors of job satisfaction. In addition to
institutional operations, quality of supervision and training,
gender also is a statistically significant predictor of job

satisfaction. Gender exerts a negative direct effect on job satisfaction, indicating that when controlling for all other variables, female detention officers express a higher level of satisfaction with their job than male detention officers.

The third model, which regresses job stress on all climate variables, is also significant, explaining a moderate proportion of variance of job stress (37 percent). Like job satisfaction, job stress is directly influenced by three climate variables. As with job satisfaction, institutional operations has a direct effect on job stress, though in the opposite direction. Higher levels of officer support for the institutional operations significantly predict lower levels of job stress. Both fear of victimization and role ambiguity have a positive influence on level of job stress, with role ambiguity exerting the greater influence on job stress. Officers expressing higher levels of fear of victimization and role ambiguity also express higher levels of job stress. The relationship between these climate variables and job stress supports previous research (Guenther & Guenther, 1974; Stalgaitis et al., 1982; Stinchcomb, 1985)

The final model, in which job stress is regressed simultaneously on all climate and individual level variables, is significant but explains slightly less variance in job stress than the previous equation. Similar to the case in predicting job satisfaction, those climate variables which exert a significant influence on job stress when only climate variables are entered into the equation remain significant even when the effects of individual level variables are controlled. Fear of victimization, institutional operations and role ambiguity continue to be significant predictors of job stress, with only a slight change in their beta weights. Unlike job satisfaction, job stress is also directly affected by education, which has a significant negative effect on job stress. Higher levels of education predict lower levels of job stress. No other individual level variable directly influences job stress.

To review, models identifying statistically significant predictors of job satisfaction and job stress reveal that individual characteristics are of little importance. When both climate and individual level variables are entered into the model simultaneously, gender is the only individual level variable to directly influence job satisfaction and education is the only individual level variable to directly influence job stress. While the effects of both gender and education may be significant, their strength as predictors is much less than that of the significant climate variables. In fact, a comparison of the amount of variance explained indicates that individual level variables add little to the prediction of a detention officer's expressed level of job satisfaction or job stress. Consequently, these findings are consistent with those reported in the literature which indicate that, although correlated with job satisfaction and job stress, individual factors explain little of the variance in officers' job satisfaction or job stress when other factors are controlled. Instead, climate factors are found to be better predictors than individual factors of officer attitudes. In this case, however, it is noteworthy that institutional operations is the only climate factor to affect both job satisfaction and job stress. Job satisfaction is significantly affected by quality of supervision and training, whereas job stress is significantly affected by fear of victimization and role ambiguity. These findings are consistent with expectations.

Table 5

Regression Analysis Summary Table For Regression of Job Satisfaction and Job Stress on Climate Variables and Individual Level Variables

	Job Satisfaction				Job Stress			
	(1)		(2)		(1)		(2)	
	B	SE	B	SE	B	SE	B	SE
Climate Variables								
Alienation	.00	.07	.03	.07	-.05	.04	-.10	.05
Authority	.02	.11	.01	.11	.02	.07	-.00	.07
Fear of Victimiz	-.05	.06	-.05	.06	.20[a]	.04	.24[a]	.04
Inst Operations	.26[a]	.05	.28[a]	.05	-28[a]	.03	-24[a]	.03
Org Support	.00	.06	.02	.06	-.00	.04	-.03	.04
Qlty of Supervsn	.19[a]	.05	.20[a]	.05	-.03	.03	-.03	.03
Role Ambiguity	-.09	.04	-.06	.05	.36[a]	.03	.37[a]	.03
Training	.14[a]	.05	.17[a]	.05	.04	.03	.05	.03
Individual Level Variables								
Male	-----		.10[a]	.40	-----		-.01	.26
White	-----		.05	.52	-----		.01	.33
Age	-----		.07	.02	-----		.02	.01
Education	-----		.00	.11	-----		-10[a]	.07
Tenure	-----		.08	.00	-----		.07	.00
Adjusted R^2	.33		.34		.37		.36	
F Ratio	36.00[a]		20.00[a]		42.00[a]		21.85[a]	

[a] $p < .01$ [b] $p < .05$

Regression of Readiness to Use Force on Individual Level, Climate and Affective Variables

The final model (see Table 6), in which readiness to use force is regressed on all individual, climate and affective variables simultaneously, explains 20 percent of the variance in an officer's readiness to use force. As noted in Table 3, not one of the individual level variables has a significant effect on readiness to use force. Of the climate variables, authority, fear of victimization and quality of supervision continue to be strong predictors, indicating that lower levels of authority over inmates and higher levels of fear of victimization and quality of supervision increase the officer's readiness to use force. However, alienation, institutional operations, organizational support, role ambiguity and training continue to exert a non-significant influence on an officer's readiness to use force. The inclusion of job satisfaction and job stress in the model (in Table 6), then, does not significantly alter the effects of the individual or the climate variables on readiness to use force (as observed in Table 3). Interestingly, job stress, though not job satisfaction, significantly influences readiness to use force. Higher levels of job-related stress increase an officer's expressed readiness to use force.

To summarize, as hypothesized, individual-level variables fail to significantly influence an officer's readiness to use force. Three of the eight climate variables and one of the two affective variables entered into the equation significantly influence an officer's readiness to use force. However, authority, fear of victimization, quality of supervision and job stress explain only 20 percent of the variance in an officer's readiness to use force. A comparison of the standardized beta weights, as well as a review of Table 3, indicate that the climate variables are responsible for the greater part of the explained variance. Yet it is clear, other factors not accounted for in this final model exert a significant influence on a detention officer's readiness to use force against inmates.

Summary and Conclusions

Principally, this analysis examines the independent effects of eight measurements of climate on a detention officer's readiness to use force. After reviewing the regression equations presented in Tables 3 through 6, the importance of climate variables as predictors of an officer's readiness to use force becomes clear. To further highlight the significance of climate, as well as summarize the key factors predicting readiness to use force, a "trimmed" model is summarized in Table 7.

This final equation includes only those independent variables found in Table 6 to have a significant direct effect on readiness to use force. Trimming the final regression model to obtain more parsimonious predictive model has little or no effect on either the beta weights of the four significant independent variables or the amount of variance in readiness to use force, which is explained by the model.

The results of this analysis of the effects of climate on readiness to use force are summarized in Figure 1. In this model, all non-significant independent variables, which have neither a direct nor an indirect effect on readiness to use force, are removed and the model is re-analyzed. This creates a parsimonious model, which includes only those variables, which are direct or indirect predictors of an officer's readiness to use force.

Of the eight measures of climate used in this study, five remain in Figure 1. Three of these climate measurements directly influence an officer's readiness to use force. Quality of supervision and authority have only a direct effect on readiness to use force, while fear of victimization has both a direct, and an indirect effect on readiness to use force, as mediated by job stress. In addition, institutional operations and role ambiguity have only indirect effects on readiness to use force via their significant effect on job stress. As noted previously, job stress, but not job satisfaction, exerts a significant positive influence on an officer's readiness to use force.

The three individual level variables, which remain in the model, have only an indirect effect on an officer's readiness to use force, with education directly influencing job stress, race directly influencing fear of victimization and tenure directly influencing institutional operations.

This trimmed model summarizes statistically significant findings and emphasizes the importance of climate in predicting a detention officer's readiness to use force against inmates. Individual level variables exert only indirect effects on readiness to use force, as do the climate variables role ambiguity and institutional operations. Fear of victimization influences readiness to use force both directly and indirectly. Authority continues to have the greatest direct influence on readiness to use force, while fear of victimization, quality of supervision and job stress more moderately influence this dependent variable.

Table 6

Regression Analysis Summary Table for Regression of Force on Individual Level Variables, Climate Variables, and Job Satisfaction and Job Stress

	Readiness to Use Force	
	B	SE
Individual Level Variables		
Male	.06	.41
White	.03	.52
Age	-.07	.02
Education	-.04	.11
Tenure	-.06	.00
Climate Variables		
Alienation	.05	.08
Authority	-.29[a]	.12
Fear of Victimization	.11[b]	.06
Institutional Operations	.08	.06
Organizational Support	-.05	.06
Quality of Supervision	.22[a]	.05
Role Ambiguity	.02	.05
Training	-.02	.05
Affective Variables		
Job Satisfaction	-.02	.05
Job Stress	.14[a]	.08
Adjusted R^2	.20	
F Ratio	9.13[a]	

[a] $p < .01$ [b] $p < .05$

85

Table 7

Trimmed Regression Model Summary Table For Regression of Force on Individual Level Variables, Climate Variables and Job Stress

| | Readiness to Use Force | |
	B	SE
Climate Variables		
Authority	-.35[a]	.09
Fear of Victimization	.11[a]	.05
Quality of Supervision	.18[a]	.04
Affective Variables		
Job Stress	.14[a]	.06
Adjusted R^2	.20	
F Ratio	37.36[a]	

[a]$p < .01$ [b]$p < .05$

Figure 1
The Trimmed Model of All Significant Direct Effects Among Variables Hypothesized to Affect Readiness to use Force.

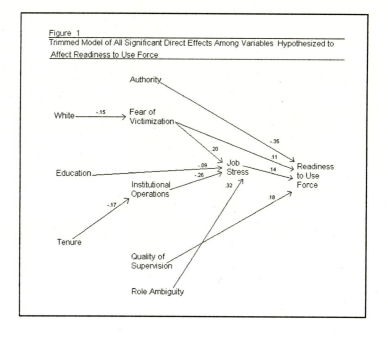

CHAPTER 6
Summary And Conclusions

Summary

Review of Literature and Findings

While a great deal of research focuses on use of force in policing, little effort has been made to explore this issue within the correctional setting. This is surprising, and generally alarming, considering that the jail is a coercive institution where the use or threatened use of force is a daily occurrence. The failure to explore further the use of force in prison and jails becomes even more troublesome in light of the nationwide trend toward equipping correctional officers with nonlethal weapons. In the absence of research on use of force by correctional officers, we must instead turn to police use of force research to examine the correlates and predictors of an officer's use of force. Generally, the literature on police use of force indicates that situational or organizational variables, and not individual level variables, are better predictors of an officer's use of force.

Although a correctional officer's use of force with inmates has not received much attention by researchers, other attitudes and behaviors of correctional officers have (e.g., stress, professional orientation, voluntary separation). Once again, it is the work environment and not individual characteristics which prove to be significant predictors of officer behavior and attitudes.

Many of these studies examining the correctional work environment can be placed under the general rubric of organizational climate research. However, such researchers often fail to frame their studies in these terms, neglecting the literature and findings from industrial and organizational psychology. As such, this study addresses these concerns and explores the concept that the behavior and attitudes of detention officers are significantly influenced by the climate within which they function. Climate is a critical link between the officer and the organization in that the way in which officers perceive conditions of the organizational environment significantly influences the attitudes and nature of their interaction with or treatment of inmates.

Findings from this analysis indicate that, as expected, the inclusion of individual level variables does little or nothing to explain variance in the eight climate variables, nor the affective variables, job satisfaction and job stress. More importantly, individual characteristics also fail to significantly influence an officer's expressed readiness to use force. However, five of the eight climate variables (authority, fear of victimization, institutional operations, quality of supervision and role ambiguity) have a significant direct and/or indirect effect on an officer's readiness to use force. Training, organizational support and alienation have no significant effect on an officer's readiness to use force.

Taken as indicators of broader climate dimensions, the relationships between the eight climate factors and readiness to use force indicate that the influence on readiness to use force does not stem from only one area or dimension of climate. Recall that the eight climate variables are placed within three broader dimensions of climate. The broader climate dimensions used in this analysis include structure and organization, comprised of three climate scales: institutional and organizational operations, training and role ambiguity. The second dimension is supervision and support, comprised of two climate scales: quality of supervision and organizational support. Finally, the third dimension, personal efficacy, is comprised of three climate scales: authority, alienation and fear of victimization.

Once again, it is interesting to note that an officer's readiness to use force is not influenced exclusively by one dimension of climate, but instead, is influenced in some way by each of these broader dimensions. After reviewing the trimmed model (Figure 1), the measures of climate which directly affect readiness to use force come from the broader climate dimensions of personal efficacy and supervision and support. The climate variables in this final model which represent the structure and organization dimension of climate have only an indirect affect on readiness to use force via job stress.

These findings suggest that an officer's perceptions of interactions and/or relationships with inmates and supervisory personnel have a more direct influence on an officer's readiness to use force than perceptions of the larger structure and organization of the institution. One explanation for this may be found in the proximity of relationships. Similar research suggests that the influence of perceived job characteristics are more significant than the organization's structured properties on employee responses to technology (Hall et al., 1978). In this analysis, perhaps the broader structure and organization of the institution is perceived by officers as far removed from their day to day functioning within the facility. Issues of supervisory support and inmate relations, on the other hand, are perceived as being 'closer' and experienced on a more regular and direct personal basis, thus having a greater influence on officer behavior and attitudes.

From this analysis, it is important to note that, contrary to the hypothesized relationship, measurements of climate did not have indirect effects on a detention officer's readiness to use force via their effects on job satisfaction. While institutional operations, quality of supervision and training are significant predictors of an officer's level of job satisfaction, job satisfaction, itself, did not significantly influence an officer's readiness to use force. It is also important to note that, without the inclusion of job stress in the final model, the influence of institutional operations and role ambiguity on readiness to use force would have gone unrecognized. More important, however, is the finding that an officer's readiness to use force is influenced by perceived job stress. Job stress, like job satisfaction, is an affective response to perceptions of climate and not a measurement of climate per se. Given the stressful nature of a correctional officer's duties and responsibilities, it is important to understand how job stress functions as a mediating variable between climate and use of force.

Once again, working as detention officer generally is believed to be a fairly stressful occupation. Research regarding the correlates of stress is ambiguous. Some studies have found a relationship between job stress and individual level variables, however these relationships are not consistent (Blau et al., 1986; Rosefield, 1981; Whitehead, 1987). Other researchers have found no relationship between individual characteristics and job stress (Blau et al., 1986; Weinberg, Evans, Otten & Marlowe, 1985;). In this analysis, only education is found to significantly influence an officer's level of job stress, with a lower level of education resulting in higher levels of job stress.

Findings regarding the influence of climate on job stress do support previous studies. Previous research on job stress generally ignores a climate framework, and instead classifies correlates of job stress as one of three types: personal factors (e.g., race, gender and tenure), occupational factors (e.g., workload, powerlessness and dangerousness) and organizational factors (e.g., departmental chain of command and supervisory practices). Studies indicate that organizational characteristics are the greatest source of job stress for correctional officers, more so than individual or occupational factors (Huckabee, 1992). In this analysis, role ambiguity and institutional operations, two variables which would be considered organizational factors under the categorization listed above, significantly influence the level of job stress. Fear of victimization, which is described as an occupational factor, also has a significant effect on job stress, though weaker than that of the role ambiguity and institutional operations. Such results do two things. First, they support earlier findings that broader issues of structure and organization have a greater influence on officer's job stress than individual or occupational factors. Secondly, these results also point to the arbitrary distinctions made among organizational variables which is characteristic of

corrections research. This is yet another example of the
failure of corrections research to frame organizational and
occupational research issues within a broader climate
framework, resulting in an often fragmented and
unorganized body of literature.

By simultaneously examining the effects of individual
level variables and climate variables on readiness to use
force, and then further examining the mediating effects of
stress and satisfaction, this research substantially extends
earlier research examining use of force in corrections.
Additionally, the extensive examination of climate research
illustrates the shortcomings of correctional research dealing
with climate factors, emphasizing the need to place such
studies in a broader framework as suggested by the rich
body of climate literature found in industrial and
organizational psychology.

Limitations of Study

Potentially the most serious, yet least assessable,
limitation to this research concerns an investigation by the
U.S. Department of Justice into the misuse and abuse of
force by detention officers in the Maricopa County jails.
During the last year of the three-year evaluation research
project from which the data for this study were collected,
the Maricopa County Sheriff's Office came under a great
deal of public and media scrutiny as the Justice Department
conducted an investigation into reported misuse of force
against inmates by detention officers. What is difficult to
measure is the extent to which this investigation by the
Justice Department influenced officer responses to the
survey instrument.

While the impact of the Justice Department's investigation on the results of this study is difficult if not impossible to determine, a number of other issues also must be weighed when assessing this situation. First, it is important to note the relationship between the evaluation team and the detention officers was established prior to any investigation or public allegations of misuse of force. The data on which this study is based come from the last of three surveys distributed to all detention officers in the Maricopa County jails over a three year period. By the time this third wave of surveys was distributed, the detention officers were very familiar with the evaluation team as we had been in the jails interviewing detention officers for approximately eighteen months. The officers understood the survey to be part of a broader evaluation of the introduction of non-lethal weapons into the jail, stemming from a research project sponsored by the National Institute of Justice and National Sheriff's Association. Also, the survey was administered with the assistance and support of the administration. More importantly, the evaluation team addressed the issue of the federal investigation in the cover letter distributed with the survey, reminding the officers of the purpose of the survey and reassuring them that the surveys were anonymous and the information collected was completely confidential. Unable to alter the potential contaminating influence of the investigation, the evaluation team attempted to allay the concerns of the officers as much as possible. The 80 percent response rate for this third survey is consistent with the response rates achieved with the first two pre-investigation surveys (72 percent in 1994 and 79 percent in 1995) and shows far more cooperation than usually noted in published studies which obtain only a 50 to 60 percent rate of response from officers. Given these circumstances, it can be argued that the findings from this study are not unduly contaminated by the outside investigation conducted during the collection of this data.

It is also important to address the political climate within which the accusations of misuse of force, the federal investigation and the subsequent collection of data for this study occurred. While some measure of confidence can be achieved as to the steps taken to minimize the contamination of the study due to the outside investigation, it is more difficult to assess the influence of the current, primarily punitive political climate on a detention officer's readiness to use force. Although not specifically identified as a factor within the research model, it is reasonable to assume that the punitive nature of the political climate in some way influences an officer's perception of the organizational climate, as well as an officer's perception of the readiness to use force. A number of models might be specified to account for the influence of this socio-political climate, but such models, which would require longitudinal data, are not the focus of this study. This remains a limitation.

A second, and more minor limitation to this study is one of generalizability. There is a need to focus on other settings, specifically the prison setting. While these findings could be applied to other jail facilities, all correctional institutions are not the same. Prisons and jails differ in many ways, including the nature of the imprisoned population and the nature of the relationship between correctional officers and inmates. Senese and Kalinich, (1993) argue, for instance, that detention officers "have more control over the climate of the facility [then do prison officers] given the higher inmate turnover rate and the resultant lack of sufficient time for the formation of a consistent inmate subculture" (p. 132). As such, it is quite possible that effects of climate on officers differs between prisons and jails and that correctional officers' attitudes toward use of force differ significantly from that of detention officers.

A third limitation to this study addresses variables found to be significant in other use of force studies, but were not collected for this analysis. Perhaps the most salient factors not included in this analysis are situational variables. Situational factors found to be significant predictors of police use of force, such as number of officers present, number of witnesses present and suspect behavior, could be adapted easily to the correctional setting.

A final limitation to this study is one which once overcome would move use of force research in corrections forward considerably. This limitation addresses the nature of the dependent variable, readiness to use force. This dependent variable is an attitudinal variable, measuring the extent to which an officer is ready to use force within the context of his or her role as a detention officer, and it does not reflect an officer's actual use of force. As a result, there is a need to move toward the construction of a behavioral measurement of use of force within the correctional setting.

Conclusions

Given these limitations, this analysis provides insight into a detention officer's expressed readiness to use force, addressing the way in which different dimensions of perceived climate influence this type of interaction between officers and inmates. The significance of this study can be seen in a number of theoretical and policy implications regarding the nature of use of force by detention officers.

First, however, it is important to place this analysis of use of force firmly within the context of the correctional setting. While the public and the media are quick to address issues of use of force only within the context of misuse or abuse, it must be remembered that jail is a coercive institution and correctional officers are agents of social control whose first obligation to the organization is that of supervision, security and control. As Williams (1983) notes:

> In order to understand the work roles and attitudes of prison officers, it is necessary to stand back from the question of what social purposes the prison as an organization ought to serve and consider the purposes that it does serve. Ideas about the prison as an agent of punishment, deterrence and rehabilitation gain and lose currency periodically. The one purpose that the prison has been constantly used for is *custody*, or segregating prisoners from the rest of society in varying degrees of confinement. (p.44)

Correctional officers are the primary agents of this organization, responsible for the control, custody and security of inmates. Such duties necessarily place the correctional officer in the adversarial role of keeper, fostering a relationship between officers and inmates which is characterized as one of "structured conflict" (Jacobs & Kraft, 1978, p. 305). The very nature of this relationship requires detention officers to remain alert, to anticipate and to respond to a variety of threatening and dangerous situations. Such a response is often in the form of use or threatened use of force. As Poole and Regoli (1980b) note,

> The guard must be ready to respond not only to actual infractions but also to potential violations. The guard therefore must maintain a state of constant alertness geared to the possibility of trouble in which the initiative rests with the inmates. (p. 216)

It is important to realize that while a competent correctional officer is required to maintain a certain level of readiness to use force as an essential part of the job, it does not represent necessarily an inherent potential for misuse or abuse.

This distinction between the legitimate readiness to use force and a more punitive conception of force associated with its misuse and abuse is important to the discussion of the theoretical significance of this study, as well as its implications for policy makers.

Theoretical Significance

As discussed above, a detention officer's readiness to use force when interacting with inmates is central to the officer's role in a correctional institution. However, the use or threatened use of force is by no means an officer's principle, nor preferred, method for gaining the compliance of inmates. In fact, research indicates that legitimate power and expert power, not coercive power, are believed by officers to be the most important reason why prisoners comply (Hepburn, 1985). With this in mind, an officer's level of readiness to use force could be interpreted as reflecting the extent to which on officer relies on a type of coercive power to control inmates. Thus, an increase in an officer's readiness to use force against inmates represents an officer's attitude toward the control and discipline of inmates.

It is not surprising then, that personal efficacy, the dimension of climate whose individual measures of climate represent the influence and ease with which detention officer's experience working with inmates proves to have the greatest influence on an officer's attitudes toward the control and discipline of inmates. An officer's perception of authority over inmates has the greatest effect on whether an officer perceives the need to use force when interacting with inmates. This feeling of authority stems from the officer's position within the organization, a position which provides the officer with the legitimate right to control the inmate. Thus when a detention officer perceives that his or her right to exercise control over inmates is diminished. the officer then feels a greater need to rely on more coercive means to control inmates.

Policy Implications

The way in which perceptions of climate function within correctional institutions and their influence on officer attitudes and behavior has significant policy implications. The importance of climate as the critical link between the individual and the organization is emphasized in industrial and organizational psychology literature suggesting that people adapt or attempt to adapt to an organization's climate, to "achieve some kind of homeostatic balance with their psychological environment" (Schneider, 1975, p. 453). Once some sort of balance is achieved, individuals may resist changes in policy or practice because they are unable or unwilling to alter climate perceptions to incorporate new information. Individuals find it necessary to ground their behavior within a broader frame of reference and, once established, are hesitant to change. Only after individuals have formed new climate perceptions will behavior change in response to organizational change, as climate perceptions "serve as a frame of reference for coherent sets of adaptive behaviors" (Schneider, 1975, p. 454).

Clearly, then, any attempt to change organizational policy and practice within the correctional institution should be made with an understanding of the significance of climate perceptions and their effect on officers' attitudes and behavior. Officers' perceived authority over inmates, which has the strongest direct effect on the readiness to use force, might be one area management would target to influence a detention officer's readiness to use force. Organizational or managerial efforts to increase the officers' awareness of their authority over inmates (and to reduce job related stress) may in turn influence an officer's assessment of a situation requiring the use or threatened use of force. To influence officers' readiness to use of force, management would need not only to implement various policies instructing officers in the appropriate use of force, but also would be wise to assess and modify, if necessary, the climate of authority that exists within the institution.

Interestingly, officers' perceptions of training do not significantly influence readiness to use force. The issue of self selection in the choice of one's occupation, and more importantly the propensity of organizations to create climates in which appropriate behaviors are learned, results in the tendency for people in a situation to behave similarly (Schneider, 1975). Use of force training is one area in which the organization has the ability to create this climate of appropriate behavior. With this in mind, one would expect a detention officer's readiness to use force to be related to a rational bureaucratic factor like training. So while a detention officer's training may teach the officer the principles of physical control, an officer's perception of this training does not significantly influence the officer's fundamental attitude toward the control and discipline of inmates.

As agents of social control, correctional officers are often forced to rely on the use of force to prevent or quell discipline problems. This fundamental reliance on legitimate use of force in the operation of correctional institutions has not been systematically examined by social scientists; nor has its potential for misuse or abuse. The absence of such research is alarming. As such, further study and examination of the routine use or threatened use of force by correctional officers in their interactions with inmates remains critical.

References

Alpert, G. P. (1989). Police use of deadly force: The Miami experience. In R.G. Dunahm & G.P. Alpert. (Eds.), *Critical issues in policing: Contemporary readings Prospect* (pp. 133-160). Heights, IL:Waveland Press.

Amnesty International (1997). *United States of America: Ill-treatment of inmates in Maricopa County Jails – Arizona* (AL Index: AMR51/51/97). London, United Kingdom.

Arpaio, J. (1994). Non-lethal weapons: The beginning. *Roundup,* February. Maricopa County Sheriff's Office.

Ashforth, B. E. (1985). Climate formation: Issues and extensions. *Academy of Management Review,* 10, 837-847.

Babbie, E. (1995). *The practice of social research.* (7th ed.). Belmont, CA: Wadsworth Publishing Company.

Barker, R.G. (1963). On the nature of the environment." *Journal of Social Issues*, 19, 17-38.

Bayley, D.H. & Garofalo, G. (1989). The management of violence by police officers. *Criminology,* 27, 1-25.

Bedeian, G.A., Armenakis, A.A. & Curran, S.M. (1981). The relationship between role stress and job-related, interpersonal, and organizational climate factors. *The Journal of Social Psychology*, 113, 247-260.

Blau, J., Light, S.C. & Chamlin, M. (1986). Individual and contextual effects on stress and job satisfaction. *Work and Occupations*, 13(1), 131-156.

Blumstein, A. (1989). American prisons in a time of crisis. In L. Goodstein & D. MacKenzie (Eds.), *The American prison: Issues in research and policy* (pp. 13-22). New York:Plenum Press.

Bowker, L.H. (1982). *Corrections.* New York:MacMillan Publishers.

Camp, S.D. (1994). Assessing the effects of organizational commitment and job satisfaction on turnover: An event history approach. *The Prison Journal* 74 (3), 279-305.

Cascio, W. (1977). Formal education and police officer performance. Journal of Police Science and Administration. 5:89-96.

Chase, M.M. (1973). *A profile of absconders.* New York:New York State Division for Youth; Research Department. World Trade Center.

Cohen, B. & Chaiken, J. (1972). Police background characteristics and performance: Summary. New York, N.Y.:Rand Institution.

Coleman, J. (1961). The adolescent society: The social life of the teenager and its impact on education. New York:Free Press, Inc.

Cressey, D.R. (1965). Prison organizations. In J.G. March (Ed.), *Handbook of organizations* (pp.1023-1070). Chicago:Rand McNally,.

Croft, E.B. (1985). Police use of force: *An empirical analysis.* Unpublished doctoral dissertation, State University of New York, Albany.

Croft, E. and B. Austin (1987). Police use of force in Syracuse, New York: 1984 and 1985. In A report to the Governor by the N.Y.S. Commission on Criminal Justice and the Use of Force. Albany, New York.

Cullen, F.T., Link, B.G., Wolfe, N.T. & Frank, J. (1985). The social dimensions of correctional officer stress. *Justice Quarterly,* 2 (4), 505-533.

De Beaumont, G. & de Tocqueville, A. (1964). *On the penitentiary* system in the United States and its applications in France. Carbondale:Southern Illinois University Press.

Deval, P.L., (1996, March 25). Formal findings letter to Ed King, Chair, Maricopa County Board of Supervisors. Re: Maricopa County Jail. Assistant Attorney General, Civil Rights Division, U.S. Department of Justice.

DiIulio, J. (1994). The question of Black crime. *Public Interest,* 117, 3-32.

Eisenberger, R., Huntington, R., Hutchinson, S. & Sowa, D. (1986). Perceived organizational support. *Journal of Applied Psychology*, 71, 500-507.

Engel, B.T. & Moos, R.H. (1967). The generality of specificity. Archives of General Psychiatry, 16, 574-581.

Etzioni, A. (1975). A comparative analysis of complex organizations. New York, NY: Free Press.

Forehand, G.A. & Gilmer, B.H. (1964). Environmental variation in studies of organizational behavior. *Psychological Bulletin*, 62, 361-382.

Friedrich, R. J. (1980). Police use of force: Individuals, situations and organizations. Annals of American Academy of Political and Social Science, 452, 82-97.

Furnham, A. & Gunter, B. (1994). Biographical and Personality predictors of organizational climate. *Psychologia*. 37, 199-210.

Fry, L.J. & Glaser, D. (1987). Gender differences in work adjustment of prison employees. *Journal of Offender Counseling, Services and Rehabilitation*, 12, 39-52.

Garland, D. (1990) Punishment and modern society: *A study in social theory*. New York, NY:Oxford University Press.

Geller, W. (1982). Deadly force: What we know. *Journal of Police Science and Administration*, 10 (2), 161-177.

Goodstein, L. & MacKenzie, D. L. (1989). Issues in correctional research and policy. In L. Goodstein & D. MacKenzie (Eds.), *The American prison: Issues in research and policy* (pp. 1-10). New York:Plenum Press.

Grant, R. (1995, May 21). Banging Up the Bad Guys. p. 6 *The Independent.*

Grennan, S.A. (1987). Findings on the role of officer gender in violent encounters with citizens. *Journal of Police Science Administration*, 15, 78-85.

Guenther, A. & Guenther, M. (1974). Screws vs. thugs. *Society* 12, 42-50.

Guion, R.M. (1973). A note on organizational climate. Organizational Behavior and Human Performances, 9 (1), 120-125.

Gump, P., Schoggen, P. & Redl, F. (1957). The camp milieu and its immediate effects. *Journal of Social Issues,* 13, 40-46.

Guzley, R.M. (1992). Organizational climate and communication climate: Predictors of commitment to the organization. *Management Communication Quarterly*, 5 (4), 379-402.

Hall, D.T., Goodale, J.G., Rabinowitz, S. & Morganm M. A. (1978). Effects of top-down departmental and job change upon perceived employee behavior and job attitudes: A natural field experiment. *Journal of Applied Psychology*, 63, 62-72.

Hayden, G.A. (1981). Police discretion in the use of deadly force: An empirical study of information usage in deadly force decision-making. *Journal of Police Science Administration*, 9, 102-107.

Hepburn, J.R. (1985). The exercise of power in coercive organizations: A study of prison guards. *Criminology*, 23 (1), 146-164.

Hepburn, J.R. (1989) "Prison guards as agents of social control. In L. Goodstein & D. MacKenzie (Eds.), *The American prison: Issues in research and policy* (pp. 191-204). New York:Plenum Press.

Hepburn, J.R. & Albonetti, C. (1980). Role conflict in correctional institutions: An empirical examination of the treatment-custody dilemma among correctional staff. *Criminology*, 17 (4), 445-459.

Hepburn, J. R. & Crepin, A.E. (1984). Relationship strategies in a coercive institution: A study of dependence among prison guards. *Journal of Social and Personal Relationships*, 1, 139-157.

Hepburn, J.R. & Griffin, M. (1998). Jail recidivism in Maricopa County: A report submitted to the Maricopa County Sheriff's Office. Maricopa County, AZ.

Hepburn, J., Griffin, M. & Petrocelli, M. (1997). *Safety and control in a county jail: Nonlethal weapons and the use of force.* (National Institute of Justice Grant 94-IJ-CX-K006). U.S. Department of Justice.

Hepburn, J. R. & Knepper, P. E. (1993). Correctional Officers as Human Services Workers: The Effect on Job Satisfaction. *Justice Quarterly,* 10 (2), 315-335.

Hershberger, S., Lichtenstein, P. & Knox, S. (1994). Genetic and environmental influences on perceptions of organizational climate. *Journal of Applied Psychology*, 79 (1), 24-33.

Horvath, F. (1987). The police use of deadly force: A description of selected characteristics of intrastate incidents. *Journal of Police Science and Administration*, 15, 226-238.

Houston, J.G., Gibbons, D.C. & Jones, J.F. (1988). Physical environment and jail social climate. *Crime and Delinquency*, 34 (4), 449-466.

Huckabee, R.G. (1992). Stress in corrections: An overview of the issues. Journal of Criminal Justice, 20, 479-486.

Indik, B. (1968). The scope of the problem and some suggestions toward a solution. In F. Berrien (Ed.), *People, groups and organizations* (pp.3-26). New York, New York: Teachers College Press.

Institute of Law and Justice (1993). *Less than lethal force technologies in law enforcement and correctional agencies.* An unpublished report submitted to the National Institute of Justice. Alexandria, VA.

Irwin, J. (1985). The jail: Managing the underclass in *American society*. Berkeley, CA:University of California Press.

Jacobs, J. (1977). *Stateville: The penitentiary in mass society.* Chicago, Illinois: University of Chicago Press.

Jacobs, J. (1983). *New perspective on prisons and imprisonment.* Ithica, NY: Cornell University Press.

Jacobs, J. and L. Kraft (1978). Integrating the keepers: A comparison of black and white prison guards in Illinois. *Social Problems, 25*, 304-318.

Jacobs, J.B. & Retsky, H. (1975). Prison guard. In Robert G. Leger & John R. Stratton (Eds.), *The Sociology of corrections* (pp. 7-19). New York: John Wiley & Sons.

James, L.R. (1982). Aggregation bias in estimates of perceptual agreement. *Journal of Applied Psychology, 67* (2), 219-229.

James, L. R., Hater, J.J., Gent, M.J. & Bruni, J.R. (1978). Psychological climate: Implications from cognitive social learning theory and interactional psychology. *Personnel Psychology, 31*, 783-813.

James, L.R. & Jones, A.P. (1974). Organization climate: A review of theory and research. *Personnel Psychology, 7*, 1096-1112.

James, L. R. & Jones, A.P. (1976). Organizational structure: A review of structural dimensions and their conceptual relationships with individual attitudes and behavior. *Organizational Behavior and Human Performance, 16*, 74-113.

James, L. R. & Jones, A.P. (1980). Perceived job characteristics and job satisfaction: An examination of reciprocal causation. *Personnel Psychology*, 33, 97-135.

Johnston, H.R. (1976). A new conceptualization of source of organizational climate. *Administrative Science Quarterly*, 21, 95-103.

Jones, A. P. & James, L.R. (1979). Psychological climate: Dimensions and relationships of individual and aggregated work environment perceptions. *Organizational Behavior and Human Performance*, 23, 201-250.

Joyce, W.F & Slocum, J.W. (1979). Climates in organizations. In S. Kerr (Ed.), *Organizational Behavior*. Columbus, Ohio: Grid.

Jurik, N. & Halemba, G.L. (1984). Gender, working conditions and the job satisfaction of women in a non-traditional occupations: female correctional officers in men's prisons. *Sociological Quarterly*, 25, 551-566.

Jurik, N. & Musheno, M. (1986). The internal crisis of corrections: Professionalization and the work environment. Justice Quarterly 3, 457- 480.

Kavanagh, J. (1994). The occurrence of resisting arrest in arrest encounters: A study of police-citizen violence. An unpublished dissertation. Rutgers University, New Jersey.

Knapp, K.A. (1989). Criminal sentencing reform: Legacy for the correctional system. In L. Goodstein & D. MacKenzie (Eds.), *The*

American prison: Issues in research and policy (pp. 111-131). New York: Plenum Press.

Litwin, G.H. & Stringer, R.A. (1968). *Motivation and Organizational Climate.* Boston: Harvard University Press.

Locke, E.A. (1976). The nature and causes of job satisfaction. In M.D. Dunnette (Ed.), *Handbook of Industrial and Organizational Psychology.* Chicago: Rand McNally.

Logan, C. (1993). Criminal justice performance measures for *prisons.* National Institute of Justice, U.S. Department of Justice; Washington, D.C.

Maghan, J. (1999). Corrections countdown: Prisoners at the cusp of the 21st century. In P. Calson and J. Garrett (Eds.), *Prison and jail administration: Practice and theory* (pp.199-207). Gaithersburg, MD: Aspen Publishers.

Manning, W. (1983). An underlying cause of burn-out. *Corrections Today* 45 (1), 20-22.

Marquart, J. (1986). Prison guards and the use of physical coercion as a mechanism of prisoner control. *Criminology* 24 (2), 347-366.

Moos, R.H. (1968). The assessment of the social climates of correctional institutions. *Journal of Research in Crime and Delinquency,* 5 (2), 174-188.

Moos, R.H. (1975). *Evaluating Correctional and Community Settings*. New York: John Wiley.

Moos, R.H. & Daniels, D.N. (1967). Differential effects of ward settings on psychiatric staff. *Archives of General Psychiatry*, 17, 75-82.

Mowday, R.T., Steers, R.M. & Porter, L.W. (1979). The measurement of organizational commitment. *Journal of Vocational Behavior*, 14, 224-247.

Murray, H. (1938). *Explorations in personality*. New York: Oxford University Press.

Niederhoffer, A. (1967). Behind the shield: The police in urban society. Garden City, NY: Anchor-Doubleday.

Patterson, B. (1992). Job experience and perceived job stress among police correctional and probation/parole officers. *Criminal Justice and Behavior*, 19 (3), 260-285.

Payne, R. (1990). Madness in our method: A comment on Jackofsky and Slocum's papers, 'A longitudinal study of climates'. *Journal of Organizational Behavior*, 11, 77-80.

Payne, R. & Pugh, D.S. (1976). Organizational structure and climate. In M.D. Dunnette (Ed.), *Handbook of industrial and organizational psychology* (pp.1125-1173). Chicago: Rand McNally.

Petersilia, J. (1990). When Probation Becomes More Dreaded than Prison. *Federal Probation*, 54 (1), 23-27.

Pierce, J. L. (1979). Employee affective responses to work unit structure and job design: A test of an intervening variable. *Journal of Management*, 5 (2), 193-211.

Philliber, S. (1987). Thy brother's keeper: A review of the literature on correctional officers. *Justice Quarterly*, 4 (1), 8-37.

Poole, E.D. & Regoli, R.M. (1980a). Examining the impact of professionalism on cynicism, role conflict, and work alienation among prison guards. *Criminal Justice Review*, 5 (2), 57-64.

Poole, E.D. & Regoli, R.M. (1980b). Role stress, custody orientation, and disciplinary actions. *Criminology*, 18 (2), 215-226.

Poole, E. D. & Regoli, R. M. (1981). Alienation in prison: An examination of the work relations of prison guards. *Criminology, 19* (2), 251-270.

Porter, L.W., Lawler, E. E., & Hackman, J.R. (1975). *Behavior in Organizations*. New York: McGraw-Hill.

Pritchard, R. D. & Karasick, B. W. (1973). The effects of organizational climate on managerial job performance and job satisfaction. *Organizational Behavior and Human Performance*, 9, 126-146.

Riksheim, E.C. & Chermak, S. M. (1993). Causes of police behavior revisited. *Journal of Criminal Justice*, 21, 353-382.

Rentsch, J.R. (1990). Climate and culture: Interaction and qualitative differences in organizational meanings. *Journal of Applied Psychology*, 75(6), 668-681.

Robinson, D., Porpino, F. & Simourd, L. (1997) The Influence of educational attainment on the attitudes and job performance of correctional officers. *Crime and Delinquency*, 43, 60-77.

Roberts, K.H., Hulin, C.L. & Rousseau, D. M. (1978).Developing an interdisciplinary science of organizations. San Francisco: Jossey-Bass.

Rosefield, H.A. (1981). Self-identified stressors among *correctional officers*. Unpublished doctoral dissertation. North Carolina State University, Raleigh, N.C.

Rousseau, D.M. (1978). Characteristics of departments, positions, and individuals: Contexts for attitudes and behavior. *Administrative Science Quarterly*, 23, 521-540.

Saylor, W.G. (1984). *Surveying prison environments*. Unpublished manuscript. Federal Bureau of Prisons, Office of Research: Washington, D.C.

Saylor, W.G. & Gilman, E. (1992). *The correspondence of objective and subjective measures of prison climate: A 'causal' analysis*. Paper presented at the 44th Annual Meeting of the American Society of Criminology, New Orleans, LA.

Saylor, W.G. & Wright, K.N. (1992). Status longevity, and perceptions of the work environment among federal prison employees. *Journal of Offender Rehabilitation*, 17 (3/4), 133-160.

Schein, E. (1990). Organizational culture. *American Psychologist*, 45, 109-119.

Schneider, B. (1975). Organizational climates: An essay. *Personnel Psychology*, 28, 447-479.

Schneider, B. (1981). *Work climates: An interactionist Perspective*. (Research Report No. 81-2). Michigan State University, Department of Psychology: East Lansing, MI.

Schneider, B., & Hall, D.T. (1972). Towards specifying the concept of work climate: A study of Roman Catholic Diocesan priests. *Journal of Applied Psychology* 56, 447-455.

Schneider, B., Parkington, J.J., & Buxton, V.M. (1980). Employee and customer perceptions of service in banks. *Administrative Science Quarterly*, 25, 252-267.

Schneider, B., & Rentsch, J.R. (1988). Managing climates and cultures: A futures perspective. In J. Hage (Ed.), *Futures of organizations*. Lexington, MA: Lexington Books.

Selo, E. (1976). Evaluating correctional and community settings. *Journal of Criminal Justice*, 4 (4), 348-350.

Selsnick, P. (1957). *Leadership in administration*. Evanston, Illinois: Row, Peterson and Company.

Senese, J.D., & Kalinich, D.B. (1993). A study of jail inmate misconduct: An analysis of rule violations and official processing. *Journal of Crime and Justice,* 19 (1), 131-147.

Sense, J. (1997, June2). US sheriff. *Agence France Press,* Domestic, non-Washington section.

Sherman, L.W. (1980). Causes of police behavior: The current state of quantitative research. *Journal of Research of Crime,* 17, 69-100.

Smith, D.A. (1986). The neighborhood context of police behavior. In A.J. Reiss and M. Tonry (Eds.), *Crime and justice: A review of research,* Chicago: University of Chicago Press.

Smith, W.C. & Ivester, T.G. (1987). The social climate of the prison: Relating initial resident perceptions to subsequent institutional adjustment. *Journal of Offender Counseling, Services and Rehabilitation,* 12 (1), 73-90.

Stalgaitis, S., Meyer, A. & Krisak, J. (1982). A social learning theory model for reduction of correctional officer stress. *Federal Probation,* 3, 33-41.

Steffens, M. (1997, September 27). America's meanest sheriff makes life difficult for prisoners. *Deutsche Presse-Agentur,* International news section.

Stinchcomb, J.B. (1985). Correctional officer stress: Looking *at the causes, you may be the cure.* Paper presented at annual meetings, Academy of Criminal Justice Sciences, Orlando, FL.

Stohr, M.K., Lovrich, N.P., Menke, B.A. & Zupan, L.L. (1994). Staff management in correctional institutions: Comparing DiIulio's 'Control Model' and 'Employee Investment Model' outcomes in five jails. *Justice Quarterly*, 11 (3), 471-497.

Stojkovic, S. (1986). Social bases of power and control mechanisms among correctional administrators in a prison organizations. *Journal of Criminal Justice*, 14, 157-166.

Sykes, G.M. (1958). *The society of captives*. Princeton, N.J.: Princeton University Press.

Tagiuri, R. (1968). The concept of organizational climate. In R. Tagiuri & G. Litwin (Eds.), *Organizational climate: Explorations of a concept* (pp.9-32). Boston: Harvard University of Press,

Toch, H. (1977). *Living in prison: The ecology of survival*. New York: Free Press.

Toch, H. & Klofas, J. (1982). Alienation and desire for job enrichment among correction officers. *Federal Probation*, 46, 35-44.

U.S. Department of Justice (1998). Prison and jail inmates at midyear 1998. Bureau of Justice Statistics Bulletin.

Van Voorhis, P., Cullen, F., Link, B.G. & Wolfe , N.T. (1991). The impact of race and gender on correctional officers' orientation to the integrated environment. *Journal of Research in Crime and Delinquency*, 28 (4), 472-489.

Walters, S. (1992). Attitudinal and demographic differences between male and female corrections officers. *Journal of Offender Rehabilitation* , 18 (1/2), 173-189.

Weick, K.E. (1979). *The social psychology of organizing.* Reading, MA: Addison-Wesley.

Weinberg, R.B., Evans, J.H., Otten, C.A. & Marlowe, H.A. (1985). Managerial stress in corrections personnel. Corrective and Social Psychiatry and Journal of Behavior Technology Methods and Therapy, 31 (2), 39-45.

Wenk, Ernst A. & Moos, R.H. (1972). Social climates in prison: An attempt to conceptualize and measure environmental factors in total institutions. *Journal of Research in Crime and Delinquency*, 9, 134-148.

Whitehead, J.T. (1987). Intensive supervision: Officer Perspectives. In B.R. McCarthy (Ed.), Intermediate punishments: Intensive supervision, home confinement, and electronic surveillance (pp. 67-84). Monsey, NY: Criminal Justice Press.

Whitehead, J.T. & Lindquist, C.A. (1986). Correctional officers' job burnout: A path model. *Journal of Research in Crime and Delinquency*, 23_(1), 23-42.

Whitehead, J.T. & Lindquist, C.A. (1989). Determinants of correctional officer professional orientation. *Justice Quarterly*, 6, 69-87.

Williams, T.A. (1983). Custody and conflict: An organizational study of prison officers' roles and attitudes. *Australian and New Zealand Journal of Criminology*, 16, 44-55.

Worden, J. (1992). The 'causes' of police brutality: Theory and evidence on police use of force. In W. Geller & H. Toch (Eds.), *And justice for all:Understanding and controlling police abuse of force* (pp.31-60). Washington, D.C.: Police Executive Research Forum.

Wright, K.N. (1979). An examination of recidivism trends in relation to organizational rather than program differences. *Journal of Offender Counseling, Services and Rehabilitation*, 4 (1), 63-80.

Wright, K.N. (1980), The conceptualization and measurement of the social climate of correctional organizations. *Journal of Offender Counseling, Services and Rehabilitation*, 4 (2), 137-152.

Wright, K.N. & Boudouris, J. (1982). An assessment of the Moos Correctional Institutions Environment scale. *Journal of Research in Crime and Delinquency*, 19 (2), 255-276.

Wright, K.N. & Goodstein, L. (1989). Correctional environments. In L. Goodstein & D. MacKenzie (Eds.), *The American prison: Issues in research and policy* (pp. 253-266). New York:Plenum Press.

Wright, K. & Saylor, W. (1991). Male and female employees' perceptions of prison work: Is there a difference. *Justice Quarterly*, 8 (4), 505-524.

Wright, K. & Saylor, W. (1992). A comparison of perceptions of the work environment between minority and non-minority employees of the federal prison system. *Journal of Criminal Justice*, 20, 63-71.

Zohar, D. (1980). Safety climate in industrial organizations: Theoretical and applied implications. *Journal of Applied Psychology*, 65, 96-102.

Zupan, L. (1986). Gender-related differences in correctional officers' perceptions and attitudes. *Journal of Criminal Justice*, 14, 349-361.

Appendix

TO: MCSO Detention Officers   July, 1996
FROM: John Hepburn

Since January, 1994, a team from ASU has been studying the use of nonlethal weapons in the MCSO jails. Over 200 detention officers have been interviewed by us about the effectiveness of these non lethal weapons, and more than 700 officers responded to our survey in 1994 and again in 1995. Now, we are concluding our study by asking for your help with the third and final survey that is being distributed to all MCSO detention officers and supervisors.

We do not work for the MCSO. Nor do we work for any federal agency that may be investigating allegations of excessive force. Instead, we are funded by the National Sheriffs' Association to work with the Maricopa County Sheriff's Office to study the effects of nonlethal weapons in the MCSO jails. The general results and conclusions about the use of the pepper spray and the stun device will be shared with the MCSO and the NSA and then published in Roll Call and other professional law enforcement journals.

We are doing this study to learn more about the reliability and effectiveness of these weapons in situations where force must be used. We also want to know how officers feel about the availability and use of these weapons and how the presence of the weapons affects the working conditions and physical safety of officers.

We are asking you and all the other officers working in the 1st Avenue, Durango, Estrella, InTent, Madison Street, and Towers jails to complete a brief survey form. Part of the survey asks basic demographic information, such as your age or sex. The other part is much longer and it asks questions about your job. For this part, there are no right or wrong answers—just answers which best describe how you feel about things at work.

This is not a test. It is just a poll of your opinions. Your responses will not be shown to your supervisor or to anyone at MCSO, so your answers will not hurt your or help you in your job. We want this to be confidential and anonymous, so please...

DO NOT PUT YOUR NAME ON THE SURVEY.

Your participation in this survey is entirely voluntary, but we hope you will fill out the survey. We don't want just a few people answering for all the rest of the officers. If you answer the questions, then your opinions will be part of our results.

After you have completed the survey for, please put it in the envelope, seal the envelope, and return it to your supervisor. Thank you!

123

Index

Organizational climate scales,
55
Organizational climate,
definition, 12, 14
Pepper spray. See Non-lethal
weapons
Pink underwear, 40, 43, 44
Poole, E.D., 37, 57, 99
Readiness to use force, 99
Readiness to use force scale,
62
Recidivism, 41, 42, 43
Regoli, R.M., 37, 57, 99
Retribution, 38, 39, 40
role ambiguity, 29, 30, 57, 68,
69, 72, 73, 79, 80, 82, 84,
90, 91, 92, 93
Role ambiguity, 29, 30, 72
Role stress, 3
Saylor, W.G., 17, 19, 20, 21,
26, 27, 28, 33, 55, 56, 58,
61
Social climate, 1, 12, 25, 30
Socio-cultural environment,
17, 21, 22, 35
Stun device. See Non-lethal
weapons
Sykes, G.M., 30, 31, 35
Tent facility, 39, 40, 41, 44
Toch, H., 26, 60

Training, 30, 45, 46, 47, 49,
57, 62, 67, 68, 69, 72, 73,
74, 75, 78, 80, 82, 91, 92,
101, 102
U.S. Department of Justice, 38,
46, 48, 49, 94
Use of force, 3, 32, 49, 98
Use of force continuum, 46
Use of force evaluation, 46
Use of force policy, 45
Use of force, and education, 9
Use of force, and gender, 9
Use of force, and race, 7, 8, 31,
63, 64, 69, 72, 73, 74, 75,
84, 93
Use of force, and tenure, 9
Use of force, attitudes toward,
10
Use of force, by detention
officer, 1, 89, 99, 101
Use of force, by police, 2, 7, 8,
9, 10, 11, 12, 31, 89, 97
Use of force, expressed
readiness, 27, 34, 47, 49,
63, 80, 82, 90, 97
Victimization, 60, 67, 68, 69,
72, 73, 74, 75, 79, 80, 82,
84, 90, 91, 93
Wright, K.N., 12, 19, 21, 23,
25, 26, 27, 28, 55